Yes, God...
I Am A Creative Woman

Shaping Your Lifestyle
and Ministry for Today's Church

Edited by
Dorothy Dahlman
and Bob Putman

Published by
Harvest Publications
2002 S. Arlington Heights Road
Arlington Heights, Illinois 60005

Copyright © 1983 by Harvest Publications
Arlington Heights, Illinois 60005
Printed in the United States of America
Library of Congress Catalog Number 83-80610

All rights reserved. No part of this book may be used or reproduced in any manner whatsoever without written permission from the publisher, except in the case of brief quotations embodied in critical articles and reviews.

"Reshaping Your Life to Three Priorities," reprinted from *Disciplines of the Beautiful Woman* by Anne Ortlund, © 1977, pps. 23-35; used by permission of Word Books, Publisher, Waco, Texas 76796.

"Portrait of a Servant, Part One" and "Portrait of a Servant, Part Two," reprinted from *Improving Your Serve: The Art of Unselfish Living* by Charles R. Swindoll, © 1981, pps. 96-124; used by permission of Word Books, Publisher, Waco, Texas 76796.

"Living Creatively," reprinted from *Ms. Means Myself* by Gladys M. Hunt, © 1972 by Gladys M. Hunt. Used by permission of The Zondervan Corporation.

"Oops! I Think I've Discovered a Gift I Shouldn't Have!" reprinted from *Prime Rib and Apple* by Jill Briscoe, © 1976 by the Zondervan Corporation.

"The Witness of Community," taken from *Out of the Saltshaker and into the World* by Rebecca Manley Pippert. © 1979 by Inter-Varsity Christian Fellowship of the USA and used by persmission of InterVarsity Press, Downers Grove, IL 60515.

"Encourage One Another," reprinted by permission from *Building Up One Another* by Gene A. Getz, published by Victor Books, Wheaton, IL.

"The Ministering Woman Employs Her Gifts," reprinted from *The Ministering Woman* by Pamela Heim, © 1980, Baptist Conference Women.

"Putting Your Gifts to Use," from *Discover Your Spiritual Gift and Use It* by Rick Yohn, published by Tyndale House Publishers, Inc., © 1974. Used by permission.

"Peace and Your Spiritual Gifts," reprinted from *Getting Control of Your Inner Self* by Dr. Rick Yohn. © 1982, Dr. Rick Yohn. Used by permission of author. All rights reserved.

"Bequest of Wings," reprinted from *Honey for a Child's Heart* by Gladys M. Hunt, © 1969 by Zondervan Publishing House.

"A Growing Single Adult Ministry Responds to Good Biblical Content," from *Single Adults Want to be the Church Too* by Britton Wood, chapter 2. © 1977 Broadman Press. All rights reserved. Used by permission.

"Evangelism and Simpler Lifestyle," taken from *Living More Simply* edited by Ronald J. Sider. © 1980 by Inter-Varsity Christian Fellowship of the USA and used by permission of InterVarsity Press, Downers Grove, IL 60515.

Contents

Preface 5
    Dorothy Dahlman
Reshaping Your Life to Three Priorities 9
    Anne Ortlund
Portrait of a Servant, Part One 25
    Charles R. Swindoll
Portrait of a Servant, Part Two 41
    Charles R. Swindoll
Living Creatively 59
    Gladys Hunt
OOPS! I Think I've Discovered a Gift
I Shouldn't Have! 73
    Jill Briscoe
The Witness of Community 87
    Rebecca Manley Pippert
Encourage One Another 103
    Gene A. Getz
The Ministering Woman Employs Her Gifts 117
    Pamela Heim
Putting Your Gifts to Use 131
    Rick Yohn
Peace and Your Spiritual Gifts 141
    Rick Yohn
Bequest of Wings 167
    Gladys Hunt
A Growing Single Adult Ministry
Responds to Good Biblical Content 179
    Britton Wood
Evangelism and Simpler Lifestyle 199
    Gladys Hunt
Afterword 213
    Dorothy Dahlman
Resources for Deeper Study 217
Notes 223

Preface

Women today are searching for experiences that express creativity in their lives. Some enroll in community classes to learn new skills, such as aerobic dance, crafts, or how to start a business. Many have entered or reentered the job market—so many, in fact, that by 1990 we can expect over 60 percent of American women to be involved in some employment outside the home.

Women are also looking for creative experience in the church. Some attend Bible studies that stress in-depth teaching and rich, individual participation. Such a class may continue for several years, until there is a sense of satisfaction and fulfillment of purpose. Other women create their own group ministries to reach out to women in the neighborhood, to senior adults (who need care or want to be involved in church life but are unable to attend), or to children, whose lives can be enriched through the influence of Christian women.

There are other evidences of this search for creative living. Each year hundreds of women attend the Christian super-seminars, Bible study conferences, district retreats and winter warm-ups, para-church sponsored conferences, and mini-retreats in the local church. No period in history has made it possible for more interesting and innovative activities to be available for women.

But a basic problem still remains—many women feel burdened by their lifestyle. Life often becomes boring, a seemingly endless fatigue of small tasks. Often women are alone and lonely, separated from parents and grandparents by miles and/or death. Some are widowed or divorced, struggling to pay a mortgage that requires larger and larger chunks of their spendable income. Who could blame anyone who feels that there must be something more to life than this?

'Yes, God...I Am A Creative Woman' is a personal encounter with authors who have undertaken this search, and discovered principles that will enable you to live and minister more creatively. The chapters that follow will guide you as you formulate a personal understanding of the role that God has designed for *you* in the building of His church. Reading is only the first step in this process, but I hope that the selections in this symposium, along with the study aids we have provided, will encourage your self-discovery in an exciting way.

'Yes, God...I Am A Creative Woman' will affirm the woman who is already involved in ministry, while encouraging others, who are seeking greater satisfaction in their lives as they develop within Christ's church.

Personal words of appreciation need to be given to the members of the Baptist Conference Women resource committee: Carolyn Carlson, Jan Bartels, Marlene Christenson, Carol Carlson and Becky Brauer. Also, Christian education staff have been an encouragement in the development of this book. Especially Jim Lemon, who helped us shape the concept, and Bob Putman, who edited the manuscript and added necessary transitional material. Each of these people pray that this book will help you accomplish your goals in creative lifestyle and ministry.

Today, reading time is at a premium. With jobs, busy lifestyles, active families and many distractions nibbling at our schedule, it is almost by force of will that we take time to read anything—and then only that which we are certain will please and/or help us. I assure you that the chapters in this collection are worth your effort. They have been carefully selected from a broad resource base, to challenge and stimulate you into the discovery and development of God's ministry in and through your life. Questions for study have been provided at the end of each chapter, and a selected bibliography has been included at the end of this book. My hope is that you will use these for personal and group study.

"What is it that God would have me to be?"

"What changes do I need to make so that I will be fully open to the workings of the Holy Spirit?"

Anne Ortlund's "Reshaping Your Life to Three Priorities," provides a scriptural answer to these questions. There are certain attitudes that God would have us develop, and He wishes us to keep these attitudes in their proper order. This is the necessary first step to becoming the woman that God would have me to be.

Reshaping Your Life To Three Priorities

by Anne Ortlund

When a sculptor starts to shape a human form from a huge lump of clay, he doesn't detail the eyes and cheekbones first. He works with the large masses, attempts to get the head proportioned to the body, to set the direction of the trunk, and so on.

As you consider your whole lifestyle, you've got to think about what your top priorities are going to be, before you decide what time you're going to get up in the morning. Let's deal with the large mass of your life first, and I want to suggest to you three priorities that can't be circumvented,[1] though they may gouge and rudely disfigure your present life-form before you get things rearranged.

God first!

You're criticizing me. I can feel it: "Too vague, too theoretical." "HODE IT, HODE IT," as our Nels says. (That's a carryover from baby talk and it's now a family expression.) Wait a minute; don't prejudge.

"Seek first His Kingdom and His righteousness, and all these [other] things shall be added to you" says the Bible (Matt. 6:33). We're to be seekers after Jesus, first. Everything else must flow out of the first. And really first! Top of the list in our lives! "The old saying of 'putting first things first' is not quite good enough. The New Testament makes it evident that the 'first' of which it speaks is a singular and not a plural; 'putting the first *thing* first' would be the only proper statement of the matter.... Anything else that might be taken out of 'all the rest' and set up as 'first' inevitably will result in doublemindedness rather than a single focus."[2]

Don't think of yourself first as a wife or a single person or a mother or a worker in some field; you will some day stand before God all by yourself.

Says Proverbs 9:12, "If you are wise, you are wise for yourself, and if you scoff, you alone will bear it." Shed all relationships, all functions from your thinking, and consider yourself first as a woman. What will God have you be and do? He will not say at the Judgment, "I excuse you from this or that because your husband didn't cooperate," or "I understand that you didn't have time to know my Word because of your job...." No one, nothing must keep you from putting God first in your life. You would have all eternity to be sorry.

We must all know intellectually and experientially that God is first. He must be our lives—in a class all by himself. Everything in our lives must converge at that one point: Christ. That's the only way we'll become integrated, focused, whole women. Jesus said, "Any kingdom divided against itself is laid waste; and any city or house divided against itself shall not stand" (Matt. 12:25). Are you divided against yourself?

The words of an anthem I wrote say it this way:

> How single, God, are You—how whole!
> One Source are You, one Way, one Goal.
> I tend to splinter all apart
> With fractured mind, divided heart;
> Oh, integrate my wand'ring maze
> To one highway of love and praise.

> O single, mast'ring Life of peace
> At Whose command the ragings cease,
> Keep calling to me "Peace, be still,"
> To redirect my scattered will.
> Keep gath'ring back my heart to You.
> Keep cent'ring all I am and do.
>
> O focused Spot of holy ground,
> Silence which is the Source of sound,
> I drop the clutter from my soul,
> Reorganized by Your control;
> Then single, whole, before Your throne,
> I give myself to You alone.[3]

I've been learning that functioning as a pastor's wife, as *Ray's* wife, or speaking, teaching, composing, writing, mothering—none of the good things in my life dare be a substitute for the best. God can have no competition in your heart, or in mine.

Are you saying, "I'm really afraid of total surrender; I've got so many dreams and plans, and I'm not sure what would happen to them if I give myself totally to God"?

The first Queen Elizabeth asked a man to go abroad for her on business.

"I sincerely wish I could, but I can't," said the man. "My business is very demanding. It would really suffer if I left."

"Sir," replied the Queen, "if you will attend to *my* business, I will take care of *your* business."

Work out the implications in your own life of putting God first. That's what this book is to help you do.

If we feel overworked and someone tells us to take a rest—that's temporary. If he tells us to go a on vacation, we'll come back afterward to the same old rat race. If he tells us to go to God, we've found a permanent solution. We'll be revolutionized. We'll go into our work rested, and remain that way.

"My presence shall go with you," God says, "and I will give you rest" (Exod. 33:14).

Let your heart go to God then! Go to him, never to go elsewhere again. Settle into him; make him your home. John 15 calls it "abiding" in him—to nestle there, secure as in a strong, eternal fortress.

We were coming home after living for three months in Afghanistan, and in a Vienna hotel I put this idea into poetry:

> From here to there, and then from there to here
> The people of this planet circling roam,
> And I, as well—but, oh, one truth is clear:
> I live in God, and God Himself is Home.
>
> From hither and from thither comes the call,
> Perhaps to places near, perhaps abroad,
> But anywhere I am, and through it all
> My heart's at home—for Home is Sovereign God.
>
> To hurry here, and then to scurry there
> May be the thing that duty asks of me;
> But oh! my heart is tranquil anywhere,
> When God Himself is my Tranquility.
>
> Yes, in my heart of heart Shekinah dwells—
> The Glorious One, the Highest and the Best;
> And deep within, I hear cathedral bells
> That call me to devotion and to rest.[4]

Dear Christian sister, do we just know God? Or do we really *know* him? The Apostle Paul, a veteran super-Christian, wrote in Philippians 3:8-10, "I count all things to be loss in view of the surpassing value of knowing Christ Jesus my Lord, for whom I have suffered the loss of all things, and count them but rubbish in order . . . that I may know Him, and the power of His resurrection." What did he mean? Let me give you Ray's explanation taken from an unedited tape just the rough, beautiful way Ray preaches, in pure Rayortlundese:

> . . . That I may know Him, and the power of His resurrection. . . ." Now, we *must* know facts *about* God, but then we must go on—go on, my friend, to the great discovery of

God himself, God himself. You see, Paul was a veteran in the faith. He was in jail for Jesus' sake. And yet he pleads that he may know God.

Friend, you were built to know God; and as you know him, and you get to know him as God himself, God himself—you come upon an ecstasy for which you were made. The facts *about* God are important. But God himself, to move into God is that for which you have been constructed.

"Get to know God!" Paul cried out!

In our first little church in rural Pennsylvania was a very old woman, the oldest person we had ever seen. Miss Ettie Neal was ninety-seven, and she was permanently in bed from a broken hip. The first time a church elder took her new blond twenty-six-year-old pastor to see her, she looked up and squeaked, "Oh, my! He's just a boy!" And truly, to her he was.

But every week Ray would go to visit Miss Ettie, and he would sit by her bed and take her bony hand in his (when she's 97 and the guy's 26, it's all right), and he would read the Bible and pray with her.

One day—now, think of this—Miss Ettie told Ray that when she was a little girl she'd gone to Washington, D.C., and had shaken hands with President Abraham Lincoln! Maybe some of you readers want to look up my husband and shake the hand that shook the hand that shook the hand. . .

Now, if someone from, say, Burma, said to me, "Do you know Abraham Lincoln?" I would say, "Certainly! He was one of our American presidents, at the time of our Civil War," and so on. But I don't know Abraham Lincoln as did Miss Ettie Neal.

And Miss Ettie didn't know Abraham Lincoln as did young Tad Lincoln, who could burst through his White House study doors any time, and climb up on those bony knees and be the recipient of his wisdom and love.

Do you see what I mean? We can know God, or we can come to *know God,* and it makes all the difference in the world.

If you set yourself to really come to know him, you'll be a rare person indeed. This is what separates the winners from the fool-around-ers: setting your face toward truly making God the number one priority of your life.

How do we do this? Let me suggest four ways; his Spirit will teach you many more.

First, practice his presence. Jesus did! He said, "Do you not believe that I am in the Father, and the Father is in Me?" (John 14:10). Yes, Jesus was special; he was part of the Trinity; but he tells us also to abide in him! So we get our clues from Jesus: when we abide continually in the Father, the words that we speak won't be spoken on our own initiative; the Father within us will do the works.

Live your life consciously before him, moment by moment. Trust him to help you do it. Psalm 16:8 says, "I have set the Lord continually before me; because He is at my right hand, I will not be shaken."

Second, jealously guard a daily quiet time spent alone with God. Jesus did! He sent the multitudes away—and prayed (Matt. 14:23). When our three babies were age 2½, 1½ and brand new, I found my days were just one succession of bottles and diapers, and I got desperate for times with the Lord! Normally I sleep like a rock, but I said, "Lord, if you'll help me, I'll meet you from two to three A.M." I kept my tryst with him until the schedule lightened; I didn't die; and I'm not sorry I did it. Everybody has twenty-four hours. We can soak ourselves in prayer, in his Word, in himself, if we really want to.

Third, seek the Lord in occasional longer hunks of time. Jesus did! In Luke 6:12 he spent an entire night in prayer, because he felt the need—he, the Son of God! How much more do we need these extended times with God? Ray and I take one day a month, usually, to go out of town and pray, think, check our schedules, evaluate where we've been, see where we're going, discuss how we're doing as a wife, as a husband. The time is all too short!

And fourth, be diligent in your attendance of public worship.[5] Jesus was! Luke 4:16 says that *"as was His custom,* He entered the synagogue on the Sabbath" (emphasis mine). Certainly the Son of God wasn't going to church "for what he would get out of it." Maybe it was often less than the best. He went because he pleased the Father in all things. Be committed to public worship of God every week whether you feel like it or not, whether the preaching is great or isn't! We go for what *God* gets out of it. He wants us to there, not via television or radio, but personally with the Body of Christ (Heb. 10:25).

The second highest priority of your life must be commitment to this very Body. That's one reason why you must never fail to worship with them. Your physical family is precious, but they are temporary—for this world only. Your spiritual family is eternal. There is much we haven't learned yet about how to function as spiritual fathers and mothers, brothers and sisters, single aunts and uncles, and daughters and sons, and we're the poorer for it. This doesn't put down that precious, unique physical family of yours; it simply raises in your thinking the level of the spiritual family! A deep prayer life with, and accountability to, some close members of the spiritual family can help make your relationship with your physical family what it ought to be.

There's a lot of talk these days which pits the church against the family—a cruel thing to do, like trying to make two friends into enemies. This kind of talk makes the church the spanking boy every time, implying that it's "spiritual" to refuse to usher, sing in the choir or teach a Sunday School class, so that we can sit home with our families in front of the television with our feet up and munch corn chips.

There is dangerous, twisted thinking here. Let me tell you about my friend Bruce's family of schnauzers. We paid a visit when mama schnauzer had her puppies. The whole family of them were in a playpen in the kitchen. The enclosure was their whole world, and those tiny pups snuggled to their mother for warmth, food, love—everything they needed.

They had no idea that they were totally dependent on a larger family, a human family—Bruce and June and their children—who were (under God) the ultimate source of the provision of all their needs.

Do you have a physical family? Then snuggle close together and enjoy the warmth, food, and love hopefully provided there. But recognize that your true source of godly love, warmth, nourishment, and togetherness should come from the larger family, the eternal family. Look carefully at the emphasis of the New Testament epistles, God's directions for us in this church age. They tell us to use our gifts to nourish the Body of Christ, and draw our nourishment from the Body, so that all the adult singles, young people without Christian parents, and marrieds without Christian spouses will feel just as cared for and loved and nourished as anyone else in God's beautiful forever-family. And when we're loved and fed and prayed for there, our lacks and needs in our physical family relationships will be wonderfully met.

Paul knew what it was to hold the family of God the highest of all human relationships. He wrote to the Philippians, "It is only right for me to feel this way about you all, because I have you in my heart. . . . God is my witness, how I long for you all with the affection of Christ Jesus. And this I pray, that your love may abound still more and more." (Phil. 1:7-9).

"Oh, boy!" we think. "Those Philippians must have been so lovable, so adorable, so wonderful—not like the Christians in *my* church!" Then we get over to chapter four and find that Euodia and Syntyche were fighting. These were good women, who were both workers for the Lord, and Paul pled with the church to find some go-between to reconcile them and keep the church from splitting apart.

Yes, the early Christians were just like us latter Christians, with all the same temptations and weaknesses, and if we're going to love each other with a true "Priority Two" kind of love, it means struggling over a threshold of pain to get there.

Gilbert Tennent was pastor of a Presbyterian church in Philadelphia around 1750, and he had the fun of pastoring a church made up almost entirely of spiritual babies saved during the "Great Awakening," a spiritual revival that swept the American colonies in the middle of the century. One of his sermons was called "Brotherly Love Recommended by the Argument of the Love of God." (We'd never title a sermon that now, because it wouldn't fit on our bulletin boards.) But Tennent knew that the need of new Christians—all Christians —is to love each other. Here's what he told them, not in 1750 Philadelphia talk which we wouldn't understand too well, but a Ray Ortlund paraphrase—again rough, unedited, right off the tape:

> He urged his congregation to love each other, and love each other to the end. He said that when you begin to love each other, you come at a certain place—oh, hear me, my friends— you come at a certain place when you discover the real truth.
>
> And in every one of our lives there's a can of worms. Believe you me! There's a skeleton in the closet of every life here. And you see, we can be known, or we can be willing to know, up to that point. That's it. That's safe—but that's superficial. But, he says, you must love right in through that painful area, right in through that painful point, love right on to the end. Refuse to let go, though you know everything about that person. Refuse to let go. He says fragile love will love up to a point— and that's not worth anything. That's what most Christians experience. But there are those who are willing to know and willing to be known, to the point where they go crashing right on through that threshold of pain, to where they really know and are known.

That, my friend—not a cup of water—is real Christian fellowship. Whatever church God has guided you to, whoever your Christian family is, get your heart together with theirs! Guard your unity! Attend to them, love them, care for them! Help them, strengthen them in God, teach them, be taught by them. And every time you're confronted by an area of painful difference, crash through!

Judy and I were in a small group of four together—meeting weekly, praying over the phone several times a week, being committed to each other at close range. Judy and I had a difference, and I guess we knew that sometime it would have to surface: Judy speaks in tongues, and I don't.

It came out one day while I was having lunch at her house, just the two of us. It became a two-hour lunch, with voices raised and interruptions—there was probably more heat than light! Bible pages were flipped and verses stabbed at, both of us trying to make our points. Finally we were hugging each other and crying, reiterating our commitment to each other through it all. And since that luncheon, there's been as much tension between Judy and me over our differing spiritual gifts, as between two sisters in a home where one has the gift of cooking and the other prefers to sew.

The third priority of our lives, after God and his people, must be the needy people of our world. We mustn't turn them off! A "God-bless-us-four-no-more" kind of life will soon make us introverted and provincial. The beautiful woman of Proverbs 31 "extends her hand to the poor; and she stretches out her hands to the needy" (v. 20).

Most people admire philanthropy, missions, and witnessing—but they leave them to the super people on whom they look with not a little awe and reverence. That's ridiculous! There are people all around us in deep trouble and desperately floundering, and they would welcome us as angels if we lent them some money, told them about Jesus, or met whatever their need happens to be.

We know this, then why don't we act? Because if you're like me, I'm naturally—well, "chicken" is the word. I need a group of Christians to whom I'm regularly accountable, to whom I can lay out the needs of those around me, and who will be responsible for seeing that I act.

One day in the beauty parlor I sat down as usual under the hair dryer and was approached by a cute redhead.

"Hi," she said, "I'm Barbara. Your manicurist quit last week, and I'm taking over her patrons."

"Hello, Barbara," I said, and five minutes later she was sharing that her husband had left her, that she was afraid of being at home alone at night, that the children all thought it was her fault and not his—soon tears were falling all over my nail polish.

"Barbara," I said, "do you go to church?"

"No," she said. "And if I don't get my head together soon something terrible is going to happen."

"Would you go with me next Sunday?"

"Of course!"

I screwed up my courage. "Would you go to an adult Sunday school class too?"

"Sure," she said, "I'll do anything!"

This was so easy, I decided to shoot the works.

"Barbara," I said, "if you really want the whole treatment, you need to do a third thing, too."

"Whatever you say," said Barbara.

"Well, you need to go to Sunday school, and you need to go to church, and then afterward you need to just hang around!"

Do you know all the wonderful things that can happen to the churchgoers who hang around afterward? The ones who bolt for the parking lot miss half the goodies. I'm thankful for my heritage of being raised by parents who were the last to leave the church, Sunday morning and Sunday evening! Even a new comer can find her way into the hearts of the people if she'll hang around!

Through the weeks Barbara followed the one-two-three formula, and there was also an invisible foundation being laid under what was happening that she knew nothing about. Every week my group of sisters would ask, "What can we pray for, for Barbara? What's happening in your relationship with her? Are you having effective conversations with her about the Lord?" And then they'd pray—with me and for me.

Well, that kind of prodding from the rear is what any Christian needs who doesn't naturally have the gift of evangelism. And so it wasn't surprising that several months later, sitting beside me in church, Barbara confessed her faith in Jesus Christ as her Savior. (Ya-hoo! Three cheers! Fireworks in heaven!)

But do you see how the three priorities must be in that order, and then how they flow into each other? Priority One must come before Priority Two. Unless we are rich in God and in His Word, our spiritual lives will be thin and we will have nothing of eternal significance to contribute to our fellow Christians. And Priority Two must come before Priority Three. Unless we are close in with our fellow Christians, the chances are we'll have little or no success in effectively reaching our world around us—maybe even our own families—for Christ.

The three priorities are such a practical part of my life now that they even affect my daily list of things to do. Often I come to a point in the day when I have choices: what's most important of the things left to be done.

I check off Priority One: have I had my daily time with God? No? Then that's next; everything else can wait. At the very least, it calls me back to an awareness of him.

I check off Priority Two: which of the remaining items on the list affect my brothers and sisters in Christ? I do them next.

I check off Priority Three. What of these items concerns my work in this world, my witness to it? They come next.

If I'm guided in my "to do" list by these three priorities, then the important takes precedence over the urgent. That's so necessary! If we live always doing the urgent, we spend our time responding to alarm bells and racing to put our fires. Ten years later we'll feel totally impoverished, because over the long haul the seemingly urgent is seldom important.

Take a good look at your life. Whatever kind of woman you are—wife, mother, career woman, single parent—have you got your priorities in order? Are you building a life of eternal consequences?

If not, like a good sculptor, you need to do some strong, radical gouging and reshaping to start making the large mass of your remaining life what you—and God—want it to be.

1. What are my three current priorities in life? Talk about these priorities with a friend. What changes would I like to make? List them.
a.
b.
c.
2. What parts of my life would have to change if I put God first?
3. Are the people in our fellowship able to share their deepest hurts without fear of ridicule or rejection? If not, what can we do to deepen their trust?
4. How often do I set apart more than an hour in God's presence? How can I schedule more?

Part of my awareness of who I am is involved with setting correct priorities. If God is my number one priority, then I am confident of my freedom and security in Christ. If I love God, then I will love and serve those who are joined to me in Christ's body, the church. If I love God and those in His Body, I must reach out to meet the needs of those who are not yet included.

The next chapter leads us farther into the discovery process. Christ has some very specific directions about what our true identity is to be. Though the Scripture passages may be familiar, the picture which they paint is probably 180° away from what we imagine when we are commended to be "servants."

"How poor is 'poor in spirit'?" "It's hard enough to smile—why should I mourn?" "Isn't gentleness out of date?" "Isn't every Christian hungry for righteousness?" You will find answers to these and other questions in Charles Swindoll's "Portrait of a Servant, Part One."

Portrait of a Servant, Part One

by Charles R. Swindoll

"What do you want to be when you grow up?"

That's a favorite question we enjoy asking children. And the answers we get usually are "a policeman" or "a nurse" or maybe "a fireman." Some kids are visionary. They answer "a movie star" or "a singer" or "a doctor" or "a professional ball player." One recently told me he wanted to be either a car mechanic or a garbage collector. When I asked why, he gave the classic answer for a nine-year-old: *"So I can get dirty!"* I smiled as I had a flashback to my own childhood. And I understood.

Let's take that same question and ask it another way. Let's imagine asking Jesus Christ what he wants us to be when we grow up. Suddenly, it's a whole new question. I honestly believe He would give the same answer to every one of us: "I want you to be different... to be a servant." In all my life I cannot recall anybody ever saying that when he grew up he wanted to be a servant.

It sounds lowly... humiliating... lacking in dignity.

In his helpful book, *Honesty, Morality, & Conscience,* Jerry White talks about the concept of serving others.

Christians are to be servants of both God and people. But most of us approach business and work—and life in general—with the attitude "What can I *get?*" rather than "What can I *give?*"

We find it encouraging to think of ourselves as God's servants. Who would not want to be a servant of the King? But when it comes to serving other people, we begin to question the consequences. We feel noble when serving God; we feel humble when serving people. Serving God receives a favorable response; serving people, especially those who cannot repay, has no visible benefit or glory from anyone—except from God! Christ gave us the example: "The Son of Man did not come to be served, but to serve, and to give His life as a ransom for many" (Matt. 20:28). To be a servant of God we must be a servant of people.

In business and work the concept of serving people must undergird all that we do. When we serve we think first of the one we are trying to serve. An employee who serves honestly in his work honors God and deepens his value to his employer. On the other hand, the self-serving employee will seldom be valued in any company.[1]

Jesus' Command: "Be Different!"

When Jesus walked the earth, He attracted a number of people to Himself. On one occasion, He sat down among them and taught them some bottom-line truths about how He wanted them to grow up. The scriptural account of His "Sermon on the Mount" is found in Matthew 5,6,and 7. If I were asked to suggest an overall theme of this grand sermon, it would be—"Be different!" Time and again He states the way things were among the religious types of their day, and then He instructs them to be different. For example:

Matthew 5:21-22: "You have heard . . . but I say to you. . . ."

Matthew 5:27-28: "You have heard . . . but I say to you. . . ."

Matthew 5:33-34: "Again, you have heard . . . but I say to you. . . ."

Matthew 5:38-39: "You have heard...but I say to you...."

Matthew 5:43-44: "You have heard...but I say to you...."

In Matthew 6, He further explains how they were to be different when they gave to the needy (6:2), and when they prayed (6:5) and when they fasted (6:16). The key verse in the entire sermon is, *"Therefore, do not be like them..."* (6:8). You see, Jesus saw through all the pride and hypocrisy of others and was determined to instill in His disciples character traits of humility and authenticity. His unique teaching cut through the facade of religion like a sharp knife through warm butter. It remains to this day the most comprehensive delineation in all the New Testament of the Christian counterculture...offering a lifestyle totally at variance with the world system.

In the introduction of Jesus' sermon, doubtlessly the most familiar section is found in Matthew 5:1-12. Commonly called "The Beatitudes," this section is the most descriptive word-portrait of a servant ever recorded.

The Beatitudes: Three Observations

Let's reread these immortal words slowly:

And when He saw the multitudes, He went up on the mountain; and after he sat down, His disciples came to Him.

And opening His mouth He began to teach them, saying, "Blessed are the poor in spirit, for theirs is the kingdom of heaven.

"Blessed are those who mourn, for they shall be comforted.

"Blessed are the gentle, for they shall inherit the earth.

"Blessed are those who hunger and thirst for righteousness, for they shall be satisfied.

"Blessed are the merciful, for they shall receive mercy.

"Blessed are the pure in heart, for they shall see God.

"Blessed are the peacemakers, for they shall be called sons of God."

"Blessed are those who have been persecuted for the sake of righteousness, for theirs in the kingdom of heaven."
"Blessed are you when men revile you, and persecute you, and say all kinds of evil against you falsely, on account of Me.
"Rejoice, and be glad, for your reward in heaven is great, for so they persecuted the prophets who were before you" (Matt. 5:1-12).

Let me suggest three general observations:

1. These are eight character traits that identify true servanthood. When all eight are mixed together in a life, balance emerges. It is helpful to realize this is not a "multiple choice" list where we are free to pick and choose our favorites. Our Savior has stated very clearly those qualities that lead to a different lifestyle which pleases Him. A close examination of each is therefore essential.

2. These traits open the door to inner happiness. Here are the fundamental attitudes which, when pursued and experienced, bring great satisfaction. Jesus offers fulfillment here like nothing else on earth. Study how each begins: "Blessed are...." This is the only time our Lord repeated the same term eight times consecutively. J. B. Phillips' translation picks up the thought correctly as he renders it "How happy" and "Happy." Those who enter into these attitudes find lasting happiness.

3. Attached to each character trait is a corresponding promise. Did you notice this? "Blessed are... (the trait) for..." (the promise). Christ holds out a particular benefit for each particular quality. And what great promises they are! Small wonder when He finished the sermon we read:

> The result was... the multitudes were amazed at His teaching; for He was teaching them as one having authority, and not as their scribes (Matt. 7:28-29.)

Never before had His audience heard such marvelous truths presented in such an interesting and meaningful manner. They longed to have those promises incarnate in their lives. So do we.

An Analysis of the Four Beatitudes

So much for the survey. Let's get specific. Rather than hurrying through all eight in a superficial manner, let's work our way through these first four qualities with care. We'll look at the next four in chapter 8. We shall be able to understand both the subtle shading and the rich color of the portrait painted by Jesus for all to appreciate and apply if we take our time and think through each servant characteristic.

"The Poor in Spirit"

At first glance, this seems to refer to those who have little or no money—people of poverty with zero financial security. Wrong. You'll note He speaks of being "... poor *in spirit* ..." (italics mine). One helpful authority, William Barclay, clarifies the meaning:

> These words in Hebrew underwent a four-stage development of meaning. (i) They began by meaning simply *poor*. (ii) They went on to mean, *because poor, therefore having no influence or power, or help, or prestige*. (iii) They went on to mean, *because having no influence, therefore down-trodden and oppressed by men*. (iv) Finally, they came to describe *the man who, because he has no earthly resources whatever, puts his whole trust in God*. So in Hebrew the word *poor* was used to describe the humble and the helpless man who put his whole trust in God.[2]

This is an attitude of absolute, unvarnished humility. What an excellent way to begin the servant's portrait! It is the portrait of one who sees himself/herself as spiritually bankrupt, deserving of nothing ... who turns to Almighty God in total trust. Augustus M. Toplady caught a glimpse of this attitude when he wrote these words that became a part of the church's hymnody:

> Nothing in my hand I bring,
> Simply to Thy cross I cling;
> Naked, come to Thee for dress,

> Helpless, look to Thee for grace;
> Foul, I to the fountain fly,
> Wash me, Saviour, or I die!³

This spirit of humility is very rare in our day of strong-willed, proud-as-a-peacock attitudes. The clinched fist has replaced the bowed head. The big mouth and the surly stare now dominate the scene once occupied by the quiet godliness of the "poor in spirit." How self-righteous we have become! How confident in and of ourselves! And with that attitude, how desperately unhappy we are! Christ Jesus offers genuine, lasting happiness to those whose hearts willingly declare:

> Oh, Lord
> I am a shell full of dust,
>   but animated with an invisible rational soul
>   and made anew by an unseen power of grace;
> Yet I am no rare object of valuable price,
>   but on that has nothing and is nothing,
>   although chosen of thee from eternity,
>   given to Christ, and born again;
> I am deeply convinced of the evil and misery of a
>   sinful state,
>   of the vanity of creatures,
>   but also of the sufficiency of Christ.
> When thou wouldst guide me I control myself,
> When thou wouldst be sovereign I rule myself.
> When thou wouldst take care of me I suffice myself.
> When I should depend on thy providings I supply
>   myself,
> When I should submit to thy providence I follow
>   my will,
> When I should study, love, honour, trust thee, I
>   serve myself
> I fault and correct thy laws to suit myself,
> Instead of thee I look to man's approbation,
>   and am by nature an idolater.
> Lord, it is my chief design to bring my heart
>   back to thee.

> Convince me that I cannot be my own god,
>   or make myself happy,
>   nor my own Christ to restore my joy,
>   nor my own Spirit to teach, guide, rule me.
> Help me to see that grace does this by providential
>   affliction, for when my credit is god thou dost cast
>   me lower,
>   when riches are my idol thou dost wing them away,
>   when pleasure is my all thou dost turn it
>   into bitterness.
> Take away my roving eye, curious ear, greedy appetite,
>   lustful heart;
> Show me that none of these things
>   can heal a wounded conscience,
>   or support a tottering frame,
>   or uphold a departing spirit.
> Then take me to the cross and leave me there.[4]

A special promise follows the trait of spiritual helplessness: "... for theirs is the kingdom of heaven," says Jesus. The indispensable condition of receiving a part in the kingdom of heaven is acknowledging our spiritual poverty. The person with a servant's heart—not unlike a child trusting completely in his parent's provision—is promised a place in Christ's kingdom. The *opposite* attitude is clearly revealed in that Laodicean congregation, where Christ rebuked them with severe words. They were so proud, they were blind to their own selfishness:

> I know your deeds, that you are neither cold nor hot; I would that you were cold or hot.
>
> So because you are lukewarm, and neither hot nor cold, I will spit you out of My mouth.
>
> Because you say, "I am rich, and have become wealthy, and have need of nothing," and you do not know that you are wretched and miserable and poor and blind and naked (Rev. 3:15-17).

Chances are good that there wasn't a servant in the whole lot at Laodicea.

First and foremost in the life of an authentic servant is a deep, abiding dependency on the living Lord. On the basis of that attitude, the kingdom of heaven is promised.

"Those Who Mourn"

Matthew, in recording Christ's teaching, chose the strongest Greek term in all his vocabulary when he wrote *mourn*. It is a heavy word—a passionate lament for one who was loved with profound devotion. It conveys the sorrow of a broken heart, the ache of soul, the anguished mind. It could include several scenes:
- Mourning over wrong in the world
- Mourning over personal loss
- Mourning over one's own wrong and sinfulness
- Mourning over the death of someone close.

Interestingly, this particular term also includes compassion, a sincere caring for others. Perhaps a satisfactory paraphrase would read: "How happy are those who care intensely for the hurts and sorrows and losses of others. . . ." At the heart of this character trait is COMPASSION, another servant attitude so desperately needed today.

Several years ago one of the men in our church fell while taking an early morning shower. As he slipped on the slick floor he fell against a sheet of glass with all his weight. The splintering glass stabbed deeply into his arm at and around his bicep. Blood spurted all over the bathroom. Paramedics arrived quickly with lights flashing, sirens screaming, and the "squawk box" blaring from within the cab. The man was placed on a stretcher as the family hurriedly raced against time to get him to the emergency ward nearby. Thankfully, his life was saved and he has fully recovered.

As I spoke with his wife about the ordeal, she told me not one neighbor even looked out his door, not to mention stopping by to see if they needed help. Not one . . . then or later. They showed no compassion by their lack of "mutual mourning." How unlike our Savior! We are told that:

> ... we do not have a high priest who cannot sympathize with our weaknesses, but one who has been tempted in all things as we are, yet without sin (Heb. 4:15).

True servants are like their Lord, compassionate.

And the promise for those who "mourn"? The Savior promises "... they shall be comforted." In return, comfort will be theirs to claim. I find it significant that no mention is made of the source or the channel. Simply, it *will* come. Perhaps from the same one the servant cared for back when there was a need. It is axiomatic—there can be little comfort where there has been no grief.

Thus far we've found two attitudes in true servants—extreme dependence and strong compassion. There is more, much more.

"The Gentle"

The third character trait Jesus includes in His portrait of a servant is gentleness. *"Blessed are the gentle, for they shall inherit the earth"* (v. 5).

Immediately, we may get a false impression. We think, "Blessed are the weak for they shall become doormats." In our rough-and-rugged individualism, we think of gentleness as weakness, being soft, and virtually spineless. Not so! The Greek term is extremely colorful, helping us grasp a correct understanding of why the Lord sees the need for servants to be gentle.

It is used several ways in extrabibilical literature:
- A wild stallion that has been tamed, brought under control, is described as being "gentle".
- Carefully chosen words that soothe strong emotions are referred to as "gentle" words.
- Ointment that takes the fever and sting out of a wound is called "gentle".
- In one of Plato's works, a child asks the physician to be tender as he treats him. The child uses this term "gentle".

- Those who are polite, who have tact and are courteous, and who treat others with dignity and respect are called "gentle" people.

So then, gentleness includes such enviable qualities as having strength under control, being calm and peaceful when surrounded by a heated atmosphere, emitting a soothing effect on those who may be angry or otherwise beside themselves, and possessing tact and gracious courtesy that causes others to retain their self-esteem and dignity. Clearly, it includes a Christlikeness, since the same word is used to describe His own makeup:

> Come to Me, all who are weary and heavy laden, and I will give you rest.
>
> Take My yoke upon you, and learn from Me, for I am gentle and humble in heart; and YOU SHALL FIND REST FOR YOUR SOULS (Matt. 11:28-29).

And what does the promise mean ". . . *for they shall inherit the earth*"? It can be understood as one of two ways—now or later. Either "they will ultimately win out in this life" or "they will be given vast territories in the kingdom, to judge and to rule." Instead of losing, the gentle *gain*. Instead of being ripped off and taken advantage of, they come out ahead! David mentions this in one of his greatest psalms (37:7-11):

> Rest in the Lord and wait patiently for Him;
> Fret not yourself because of him who prospers in his way,
> Because of the man who carries out wicked schemes.
> Cease from anger, and forsake wrath;
> Fret not yourself, it leads only to evildoing.
> For evildoers will be cut off,
> But those who wait for the Lord, they will inherit the land.
> Yet a little while and the wicked man will be no more;
> And you will look carefully for his place, and he will not be there.
> But the humble will inherit the land,
> And will delight themselves in abundant prosperity.

See the contrast?

From all outward appearance it seems as though the wicked win out. They prosper in their way, their schemes work, their cheating and lying and unfair treatment of others appear to pay off. They just seem to get richer and become more and more powerful. As James Russell Lowell once put it:

> Truth forever on the scaffold
> Wrong forever on the throne.

But God says it won't be "forever." The ultimate victory will *not* be won by the wicked. "The gentle" will win. Believe that, servant-in-the-making! Be different from the system! Stay on the scaffold . . . trust your heavenly Father to keep His promise regarding your inheritance. It is you who will be blessed.

Before closing this chapter. I want us to consider another character trait of a servant—the fourth in the list of eight.

"Those Who Hunger and Thirst for Righteousness"

The true servant possesses an insatiable appetite for what is right, a passionate drive for justice. Spiritually speaking, the servant is engaged in a pursuit of God . . . a hot, restless, eager longing to walk with Him, to please Him.

Eleventh-century Bernard of Clairveaux expressed it in this way in his hymn, *Jesus, Thou Joy of Loving Hearts:*

> We taste Thee, O thou living Bread,
> And long to feast upon Thee still;
> We drink of Thee, the Fountainhead,
> And thirst our souls from Thee to fill.[5]

Bernard's pen dripped with that insatiable appetite for God.

But there is a practical side of this fourth beatitude as well. It includes not just looking upward, pursuing a vertical holiness, but also looking around and being grieved over the corruption, the inequities, the gross lack of integrity, the moral compromises that abound. The servant "hungers and thirsts" for right on earth. Unwilling simply to sigh and shrug off the lack of justice and purity as inevitable, servants press on for righteousness. Some would call them idealists or dreamers.

One such person was Dag Hammarskjold, former Secretary General of the United Nations, who died in a tragic airplane crash while flying over northern Rhodesia on a mission to negotiate a cease fire. In his fine book, *Markings,* the late statesman wrote:

> Hunger is my native place in the land of the passions. Hunger for fellowship, hunger for righteousness—for a fellowship founded on righteousness, and a righteousness attained in fellowship.
>
> Only life can satisfy the demands of life. And this hunger of mine can be satisfied for the simple reason that the nature of life is such that I can realize my individuality by becoming a bridge for others, a stone in the temple of righteousness.
>
> Don't be afraid of yourself, live your individuality to the full—but for the good of others. Don't copy others in order to buy fellowship, or make convention your law instead of living the righteousness.
>
> To become free and responsible. For this alone was man created. . . .[6]

And what will happen when this passionate appetite is a part of one's life? What does Jesus promise?

. . .they shall be satisfied.

A. T. Robertson, a Greek scholar of yesteryear, suggests the term *satisfied* is commonly used for feeding and fattening cattle, since it is derived from the term for fodder or grass? What a picture of contentment! Like well-fed, hefty livestock . . . contented in soul and satisfied within, the servant with an appetite for righteousness will be filled. It's comforting to hear that promise. Normally, one would think such an insatiable pursuit would make one so intense there would be only fretfulness and agitation. But, no, Jesus promises to bring a satisfaction to such hungry and thirsty souls . . . a "rest" of spirit that conveys quiet contentment.

1. What reservations do I hold about being a servant? What person or group of people would I rather not be asked to serve?
2. Which of the beatitudes makes me uncomfortable? Why?
3. How do I build up the self-esteem and dignity of others, even when I want to feel resentful or hurt?
4. In what ways do I show the characteristics of the four beatitudes explained in this chapter? In what ways would I like to change?

"Therefore, do not be like them . . ." Jesus said. He wants us to be different from those who do not know Him. He wants us to be servants to all.

But what is a servant like? She places all of her confidence, all of her trust in the grace of Jesus Christ, her Savior. She has an honest, passionate lament about the wrongs and hurts of those around her. She has a calm, controlled, soothing effect in tepid situations. She desires to be with God and to please Him.

But this is only part of the portrait. According to Matthew 5:1-12, there are four more characteristics of a true servant. As we look at these, and the promises which Christ attaches to them, let's consider, "How different am I, really?"

Portrait of a Servant, Part Two

by Charles R. Swindoll

You don't run through an art gallery; you walk very slowly. You often stop, study the treasured works of art, taking the time to appreciate what has been painted. You examine the texture, the technique, the choice and mixture of colors, the subtle as well as the bold strokes of the brush, the shadings. And the more valuable the canvas, the more time and thought it deserves. You may even return to it later for a further and deeper look, especially if you are a student of that particular artist.

In the gallery of His priceless work, the Lord God has included a portrait of vast value. It is the portrait of a servant carefully painted in words that take time to understand and appreciate. The frame in which the portrait has been placed is Jesus Christ's immortal Sermon on the Mount. We have examined a portion of the portrait already, but we are returning for another look, hoping to see more that will help us become the kind of persons the artist has portrayed.

Analysis of Four More Qualities

In His word-portrait of a servant, Christ emphasizes eight characteristics or qualities. We have studied the first four in the previous chapter. We now return to the picture for an analysis of the final four.

> Blessed are the merciful, for they shall receive mercy.
> Blessed are the pure in heart, for they shall see God.
> Blessed are the peacemakers, for they shall be called sons of God.
> Blessed are those who have been persecuted for the sake of righteousness, for theirs is the kingdom of heaven.
> Blessed are you when men revile you, and persecute you, and say all kinds of evil against you falsely, on account of Me.
> Rejoice, and be glad, for your reward in heaven is great, for so they persecuted the prophets who were before you (Matt. 5:7-12).

"The Merciful"

Mercy is concern for people in need. It is ministry to the miserable. Offering help for those who hurt . . . who suffer under the distressing blows of adversity and hardship. The term itself has an interesting background.

> It does not mean only to sympathise with a person in the popular sense of the term; it does not mean simply to feel sorry for someone in trouble. *Chesedh, mercy,* means the ability to get right inside the other person's skin. . . . Clearly this is much more than an emotional wave of pity; clearly this demands a quite deliberate effort of the mind and of the will. It denotes a sympathy which is not given, as it were, from outside, but which comes from a deliberate identification with the other person, until we see things as he sees them, and feel things as he feels them.[1]

Those special servants of God who extend mercy to the miserable often do so with much encouragement because they identify with the sorrowing—they "get inside their skin." Rather than watching from a distance or keeping the needy safely at arm's length, they get in touch, involved, and offer assistance that alleviates some of the pain.

A large group of the collegians in our church in Fullerton, California, pile into our bus one weekend a month and travel together—not to a mountain resort or the beach for fun-n-games, but to a garbage dump in Tijuana, Mexico, where hundreds of poverty-stricken Mexican families live. Our young adults, under the encouraging leadership of Kenneth Kemp (one of our pastoral staff team members), bring apples and other foodstuff, plus money they have collected to share with those in that miserable existence. There are times when the students can hardly believe what they see and hear *and smell* as they witness raw, unmasked poverty in the garbage dump at Tijuana.

What are they doing? They are showing mercy . . . a ministry to others that is born out of the womb of identification. In our isolated, cold society, mercy is rarely demonstrated. Shocking stories make headlines today with remarkable regularity.

A young woman was brutally attacked as she returned to her apartment late one night. She screamed and shrieked as she fought for her life . . . yelling until she was hoarse. . . for thirty minutes . . . as she was beaten and abused. Thirty-eight people watched the half-hour episode in rapt fascination from their windows. Not one so much as walked over to the telephone and called the police. She died that night as thirty-eight witnesses stared in silence.

Another's experience was similar. Riding on a subway, a seventeen-year-old youth was quietly minding his own business when he was stabbed repeatedly in the stomach by attackers. Eleven riders watched the stabbing, but none came to assist the young man. Even after the thugs had fled and the train had pulled out of the station and he lay there in a pool of his own blood, not one of the eleven came to his side.

Less dramatic, but equally shocking, was the ordeal of a lady in New York City. While shopping on Fifth Avenue in busy Manhattan, this lady tripped and broke her leg. Dazed, anguished, and in shock she called out for help. Not for two minutes. Not for twenty minutes. But for *forty* minutes, as shoppers and business executives, students and merchants walked around her and stepped over her, completely ignoring her cries. After literally hundreds had passed by, a cab driver finally pulled over, hauled her into his taxi, and took her to a local hospital.

> If you had a friend who is in need . . . and you say to him, "Well, good-bye and God bless you; stay warm and eat hearty," and then don't give him clothes or food, what good does that do? (James 2:15-16,TLB).

The apostle John probes even deeper when he asks:

> . . . if someone who is supposed to be a Christian . . sees a brother in need, and won't help him—how can God's love be within him? (1 John 3:17, TLB).

True servants are merciful. They care. They get involved. They get dirty, if necessary. They offer more than pious words.

And what do they get in return? What does Christ promise? *". . . they shall receive mercy."* Those who remain detached, distant, and disinterested in others will receive like treatment. But God promises that those who reach out and demonstrate mercy will, in turn, receive it. Both from other people as well as from God Himself. We could paraphrase this beatitude: "O the bliss of one who identifies with and assists others in need—who gets inside their skin so completely he sees with their eyes and thinks with their thoughts and feels with their feelings. The one who does that will find that others do the same for him when he is in need."

That is exactly what Jesus, our Savior, did for us when He came to earth. By becoming human, He got right inside our skin, literally. That made it possible for Him to see life through our eyes, feel the sting of our pain, and identify with the anguish of human need. He understands. Remember those great words:

> But Jesus the Son of God is our great High Priest who has gone to heaven itself to help us; therefore let us never stop

trusting him. This High Priest of ours understands our weaknesses, since he had the same temptations we do, though he never once gave way to them and sinned (Heb. 4:14-15, TLB).

"The Pure in Heart"

Like the first characteristic—"poor in spirit" (v.3)—this quality emphasizes the inner man . . . the motive . . . the "heart." It does not refer simply to doing the right things, but doing the right things *for the right reason.* Being free from duplicity, hypocrisy, and/or sham. God desires His servants to be "real" people—authentic to the core. The portrait He paints is realistic.

In Jesus' day many of the religious authorities who claimed to serve the people were not "pure in heart." Far from it! Hypocritical and phony, they played a role that lacked internal integrity. In Matthew 23—one of the most severe rebukes against hypocrisy in all the Bible—we find words in strong contrast with the beatitudes. Instead of eight "Blessed are yous," there are eight "Woe unto yous." Count them—Matthew 23:13, 14, 15, 16, 23, 25, 27, and 29!

Woe unto whom? Well, read verses 25-28.

> Woe to you, scribes and Pharisees, hypocrites! For you clean the outside of the cup and of the dish, but inside they are full of robbery and self-indulgence.
>
> You blind Pharisee, first clean the inside of the cup and of the dish, so that the outside of it may become clean also.
>
> Woe to you, scribes and Pharisees, hypocrites! For you are like whitewashed tombs which on the outside appear beautiful, but inside they are full of dead men's bones and all uncleanness.
>
> Even so you too outwardly appear righteous to men, but inwardly you are full of hypocrisy and lawlessness.

Wow, *Jesus* said that! It is doubtful He despised anything among those who claimed to serve God more than hypocrisy—a lack of purity of heart. Did you notice what characterized the phony Pharisees?

- They were big on rules and little on godliness.
- They were big on externals and little on internals.
- They were big on public commands and little on personal obedience.
- They were big on appearance and little on reality.

On the outside they "appeared righteous to men," but inwardly they were "full of dead men's bones . . . full of hypocrisy." Why did he hate that so much? Because it represented the antithesis of servanthood. Time after time, therefore, He announced, "Woe to you. . . !"

Back to Matthew 5:8—the "pure in heart." Jesus extols this virtue. The term *pure* literally means "clean." It's the idea of being uncontaminated, without corruption or alloy. Without guile . . . sincere and honest in motive.

I love the story of the well-respected British pastor who, many years ago, took the trolley early Monday morning from his home in the suburbs to his church in the downtown section of London. He paid the driver as he got on, preoccupied with his busy schedule and the needs of his large congregation. It wasn't until he was seated that he realized the driver had given him too much change. Fingering the coins, his first thought was an alien one, "My, how wonderfully God provides!" But the longer he sat there, the less comfortable he became. His conscience telegraphed a strong signal of conviction within him. As he walked to the door to get off near his parish, he looked at the driver and quietly said, "When I got on, you accidentally gave me too much change."

The driver, with a wry smile, replied, "It was no accident at all. You see, I was in your congregation yesterday and heard your sermon on honesty. I just thought I'd put you to the test, Reverend."

Christ promises the consistent servants who are pure in heart "shall see God." There is no doubt about the destiny of these individuals. For sure, some glorious day in the future, these servants will see the Lord and hear the most significant words that will ever enter human ears: ". . . Well done, good and faithful slave; you were faithful . . . enter into the joy of your master" (Matt. 25:21).

Before we move on to the next servant quality, let me challenge you to become "pure in heart." Think about what it would mean, what changes you would have to make, what habits you'd have to break. . . most of all, what masks you'd have to peel off.

As I write these words, my family and I are spending Thanksgiving week high up in the Rockies at a ski resort in Keystone, Colorado. I was invited to speak to about five hundred single career people. Many of them are on the Campus Crusade for Christ staff. What a great bunch! All week I have been talking about servanthood (sound familiar?) and emphasizing being real, authentic, pure-in-heart people. We've discussed our tendency to cover up, to say one thing and mean another, to be downright hypocritical—yet in such a clever way that nobody knows it.

Last night I decided to try something I had never done before to drive the point home. At my last birthday my sister gave me a full-face rubber mask. . . one of those crazy things that slip over your entire head. She told me she'd give me ten dollars if I'd wear it into the pulpit one Sunday (my kids raised it to fifteen dollars), but I just couldn't do it! Well, last night I wore that ugly beast when I got up to speak. I figured if any body could handle it, this gang could. *It was wild!*

I didn't call attention to it. Without any explanation, I just stood up and began to speak on being authentic. There I stood pressing on, making one statement after another as the place came apart at the seams. Why? Anybody knows why! My mask canceled out everything I had to say, especially on *that* subject. It's impossible to be very convincing while you wear a mask.

I finally pulled the thing off and the place settled down almost immediately. As soon as it did, everybody got the point. It's a funny thing, when we wear *literal* masks, nobody is fooled. But how easy it is to wear invisible ones and fake people out by the hundreds week after week. Did you know that the word *hypocrite* comes from the ancient Greek plays? An actor would place a large, grinning mask in front of his face and quote his comedy lines as the audience would roar with laughter. He would then slip backstage and grab a frowning, sad, oversized mask and come back quoting tragic lines as the audience would moan and weep. Guess what he was called. A *hupocritos,* one who wears a mask.

Servants who are "pure in heart" have peeled off their masks. And God places special blessing on their lives.

"The Peacemakers"

Interestingly, this is the only time in all the New Testament that the Greek term translated "peacemakers" appears. Maybe it will help us understand the meaning by pointing out first what it does not mean.

- It does not mean, "Blessed are those who avoid all conflict and confrontations."
- Neither does it mean, "Blessed are those who are laid back, easygoing, and relaxed."
- Nor, "Blessed are those who defend a 'peace at any price' philosophy."
- It doesn't mean, "Blessed are the passive, those who compromise their convictions when surrounded by those who would disagree."

No, none of those ideas are characteristics of the "peacemaker" in this verse.

The overall thrust of Scripture is the imperative, "Make peace!" Just listen:

> If possible, so far as it depends on you, be at peace with all men (Rom. 12:18).

So then let us pursue the things which make for peace and the building up of one another (Rom. 14:19).

For where jealousy and selfish ambition exist, there is disorder and every evil thing.

But the wisdom from above is first pure, then peaceable, gentle, reasonable, full of mercy and good fruits, unwavering, without hypocrisy.

And the seed whose fruit is righteousness is sown in peace by those who make peace.

What is the source of quarrels and conflicts among you? Is not the source your pleasures that wage war in your members?

You lust and do not have; so you commit murder. And you are envious and cannot obtain; so you fight and quarrel (James 3:16-4:2).

Get the picture? A "peacemaker" is the servant who . . . First, is at peace with himself—internally, at ease . . . not agitated, ill-tempered, in turmoil . . . and therefore not abrasive. Second, he/she works hard to settle quarrels, not start them . . . is accepting, tolerant, finds no pleasure in being negative.

In the words of Ephesians 4:3, peacemakers ". . . preserve the unity of the Spirit in the bond of peace."

Ever been around Christians who are *not* peacemakers? Of course. Was it pleasant? Did you sense a servant's heart? Were you built up and encouraged . . . was the body of Christ strengthened and supported? You know the answers.

In Leslie Flynn's potent book *Great Church Fights* (I like that title), he does a masterful job of describing just how petty and abrasive we can become. He includes an anonymous poem that bites deeply into our rigid intolerance. Our tendency toward exclusiveness is exposed for all to see:

> Believe as I believe, no more, no less;
> That I am right, and no one else, confess;
> Feel as I feel, think only as I think;
> Eat what I eat, and drink but what I drink;

> Look as I look, do always as I do;
> And then, and only then, I'll fellowship with you.[2]
> Source Unknown

Whoever lives by that philosophy does not qualify as a peacemaker, I can assure you.

But enough of the negative! Solomon gives us wise counsel on some of the things peacemakers do:

- **They build up.** "The wise woman builds her house..." (Prov. 14:1).
- **They watch their tongues and heal rather than hurt.** "A gentle answer turns away wrath..." (Prov. 15:1). "Pleasant words are a honeycomb, sweet to the soul and healing to the bones" (Prov. 16:24).
- **They are slow to anger.** "A hot-tempered man stirs up strife, but the slow to anger pacifies contention" (Prov. 15:18). "He who is slow to anger is better than the mighty, and he who rules his spirit, than he who captures a city" (Prov. 16:32).
- **They are humble and trusting.** "An arrogant man stirs up strife, but he who trusts in the lord will prosper" (Prov. 28:25).

The Lord Jesus states a marvelous promise that peacemakers can claim: "... they shall be called sons of God." God's children. Few things are more godlike than *peace*. When we promote it, pursue it, model it, we are linked directly with Him.

A man I have admired for two decades, the man who taught me Hebrew in seminary many years ago, is Dr. Bruce Waltke. He is not only a Semitic scholar *par excellence,* he is a gracious servant of our Lord. In my opinion, he is one of the finest examples of a peacemaker in the family of God. Too brilliant for words, yet the epitome of grace and love. What a magnificent balance!

A number of years ago, Dr. Waltke, another pastor, a graduate student at Brandeis University (also a seminary graduate), and I toured the mother church of the First Church of Christ Scientist in downtown Boston. The four of us were completely anonymous to the elderly lady who smiled as we entered. She had no idea she was meeting four evangelical ministers—and we chose not to identify ourselves, at least at first.

She showed us several interesting things on the main floor. When we got to the multiple-manual pipe organ, she began to talk about their doctrine and especially their belief about no judgment in the life beyond. Dr. Waltke waited for just the right moment and very casually asked:

"But, Ma'am doesn't it say somewhere in the Bible 'It is appointed unto man once to die and after that, the judgment'?" He could have quoted Hebrews 9:27 in Greek! But he was so gracious, so tactful with the little lady. I must confess, I stood back thinking, "Go for it, Bruce. Now we've got her where we want her!"

The lady, without a pause, said simply, "Would you like to see the second floor?"

You know what Dr. Waltke said? "We surely would, thank you."

She smiled, somewhat relieved, and started to lead us up a flight of stairs.

I couldn't believe it! All I could think was, "No, don't let her get away. Make her answer your question!" As I was wrestling within, I pulled on the scholar's arm and said in a low voice, "Hey, why didn't you nail the lady? Why didn't you press the point and not let her get away until she answered?"

Quietly and calmly he put his hand on my shoulder and whispered, "But, Chuck, that wouldn't have been fair. That wouldn't have been very loving, either—now would it?"

Wham! The quiet rebuke left me reeling. I shall *never* forget that moment. And to complete the story, you'll be interested to know that in less than twenty minutes he was sitting with the woman alone, tenderly and carefully speaking with her about the Lord Jesus Christ. She sat in rapt attention. He, the gracious peacemaker, had won a hearing. And I, the scalpsnatcher, had learned an unforgettable lesson.

Do you know what she saw in my friend? A living representation of one of God's . . . exactly as God promised in his beatitude . . . *"they shall be called sons of God."*

In this chapter we have been examining a portrait. We have seen the servant as merciful, authentic, and one who actively pursues peace. There remains one final part of the picture we need to linger over and appreciate.

"Those Who Have Been Persecuted"

I don't know how this strikes you, but it seems misplaced at first glance. Especially on the heels of what we just learned about being peacemakers. But it is not misplaced. Realistically, wrong treatment often comes upon those who do what is *right*. I deal with this at length in chapter 12. We who genuinely desire to serve others soon discover that being mistreated isn't the exception. It's the rule! Christ knew that was so. Read the verses carefully.

> Blessed are those who have been persecuted for the sake of righteousness, for theirs is the kingdom of heaven.
> Blessed are you when men revile you, and persecute you, and say all kinds of evil against you falsely, on account of Me.
> Rejoice, and be glad, for your reward in heaven is great, for so they persecuted the prophets who were before you (Matt. 5:10-12).

Did you notice something? Not "if" men revile you . . . but "when" they revile you. And not only will they revile you, they will persecute you and say all kinds of evil against you—lies and slanderous accusations. Clearly, Jesus is speaking of being viciously mistreated. It's tough to bear! But the Savior says you will be "blessed" when you endure it—promising a great reward for your patient, mature endurance. There are times when the only way servants can make it through such severe times without becoming bitter is by focusing on the ultimate rewards that are promised. Jesus even says we are to "rejoice and be glad" as we think on the great rewards He will give to us in heaven.

Charles Haddon Spurgeon remains one of the most colorful and gifted preachers in the history of the church. Any man who loves to preach and desires to cultivate the art and skill of communication must study Spurgeon. Before the man was thirty, he was the most popular preacher in England. The new Tabernacle was filled to overflowing every Lord's Day as people came miles by horse and buggy to hear the gifted man handle the Word of God. They were challenged, encouraged, exhorted, fed, and built up in the Christian faith. He was truly a phenomenon. As a result, he became the object of great criticism by the press, by other pastors, by influential people in London, and by petty parishioners. The man, not always a model of quiet piety (to say the least), had numerous enemies. Normally, he handled the criticism fairly well . . . but finally it began to get to him. He began to slump beneath the attacks. The persecution started to take a severe toll on his otherwise resilient spirit.

I am told that his wife, seeing the results of those verbal blows on her husband, decided to assist him in getting back on his feet and regaining his powerful stature in the pulpit. She found in her Bible Matthew 5:10-12—the beatitude we have been studying—and she printed in beautiful old English the words of this passage on a large sheet of paper. Then she tacked that sheet to the ceiling of their bedroom, directly above Charles' side of the bed! Every morning, every evening, when he would rest his enormous frame in his bed, the words were there to meet and to encourage him.

> Blessed are those who have been persecuted for the sake of righteousness, for theirs is the kingdom of heaven.
> Blessed are you when men revile you, and persecute you, and say all kinds of evil against you falsely, on account of Me.

Rejoice, and be glad, for your reward in heaven is great, for so they persecuted the prophets who were before you.

The large sheet of paper remained fixed to the ceiling for an extended period of time until it had done the job. May Mrs. Spurgeon's tribe increase! It is refreshing to think how a marriage partner can be such a vital channel of encouragement.

And it is also encouraging to see that we have no corner on the problem of persecution. Did you observe what Christ said? ". . . so they persecuted the prophets who were before you." Servants, that statement will help us call a halt to the next pity party we are tempted to throw for ourselves. We are not alone. It has been going on for centuries.

A Last Look at the Portrait

Shortly before her death in February of 1971, my mother did an oil painting for me. It has become a silent "friend" of mine, a mute yet eloquent expression of my calling. It is a picture of a shepherd with his sheep. The man is standing all alone with his crook in his hand, facing the hillside with sheep here and there. You cannot see the shepherd's face, but the little woolies surrounding him have personalities all their own. Some have the appearance of being devoted and loving, one looks independent and stubborn, another is starting to wander in the distance. But the shepherd is there with his flock, faithfully and diligently tending them.

The rather large piece of art hangs in my study with a light above it. There are occasions when I am bone weary after a huge day of people demands, preaching, and close contact with the Fullerton flock. Occasionally on days like this, I will turn off my desk lamp and my light overhead and leave on only the light on that unique painting. It helps me keep my perspective. It is a reminder . . . a simple, silent affirmation that I am right where God wants me, doing the very things He wants me to do. There is something very encouraging about taking a final look at the shepherd with his sheep at the end of my day.

We have done that in these two chapters. With a close eye on details, we have studied a portrait Jesus painted of a servant. And we have found it to be both enlightening and encouraging. We have found His promises to be assuring and His repeated reminders ("Blessed are . . .") to be affirming. He described our calling by explaining our role as:

- Poor in spirit
- Mourning
- Gentle
- Hungering and thirsting for righteousness
- Merciful
- Pure in heart
- Peacemakers
- Persecuted

As we have turned out all other lights that distract us, it has helped to concentrate our full attention on these eight specifics. In our tasteless, dark world, servants actually become the only source of salt and light.

1. What are my motives for seeking fellowship? For the purchases I make? For giving to specific charities that I presently help? For reading this book?
2. Am I at peace with myself? Am I content with who I am at this point in my life?
3. When am I most critical towards others? What triggers this critical spirit in me?
4. In what ways do I show the characteristics of the four beatitudes explained in this chapter? In what ways would I like to change?

A true servant is merciful, she is involved in meeting the real needs of the miserable. She has removed her invisible masks. She pursues peace in all her relations and honestly accepts that she will suffer for her living witness for Jesus Christ. She is different from those who are in the world.

"Great, so I know God's priorities and the characteristics of the servant which he desires me to be. I'm not Wonder Woman. How am I supposed to become that impossible person you've just described?"

Our God is a creative God, with immense powers: "For nothing will be impossible with our God" (Luke 1:37). He makes the blind to see, the lame to walk and the dead to rise up from the grave. He stretches us and directs our steps so that we may grow. He stirs the Michelangelo, the Mother Theresa, the creative "me" in all of us.

"Am I dreaming dreams which will enable me to grow?"
"Is my life an adventure?"

Living Creatively

by Gladys Hunt

Two little brothers shared the same room, and every night the smallest one fell out of bed, arousing the whole household in his trauma. It happened so often that the events became breakfast-time conversation. After listening quietly for some time, the older boy finally offered his opinion, "Want to know why Timmy falls out of his bed every night? . . .He goes to sleep too close to where he gets in."

Many people have Timmy's problem. They go to sleep too close to where they got in. Dull of spirit, they feel uninteresting and act that way, too, because they went to sleep where they were, and life has grown smaller and smaller.

If I were to ask you how much wealth you had gained in the last five years, what would you say? Inner wealth, I mean. The furnishings inside that are beautiful, interesting and enriching to others. Some people are like the two men I saw in a cartoon: one said to the other, "By the time I was smart enough to know where I was going I wasn't going any place."

Of all people in the world, the people who claim to know God best ought to be the most creative simply because they are related to the Creator. He is the innovator, the creator, the artist. Imagination finds its source in him!

Imagine being there when "the morning stars sang together" as the world was created by the word of his power. He shaped birds with their various plumage; he designed the hippopotamus and the giraffe. Light, dark, sun, moon, water, sky, clouds, earth, trees—the rose. And man in his own image.

He let Adam be a word partner with him by naming the animals. He designed the high priest's robe and the mercy seat, and equipped the artisans with his Holy Spirit. He told Solomon how to carve out the lilies at the top of the columns in the temple. This is our God.

God, the creative Redeemer—who invades our planet to deliver us from our sins and the fear of death—comes not with trumpets and royal fanfare, but as a baby. God, the adventurer.

Did you know that twenty-five percent of the Bible is poetry? In the last part of Job when God speaks he gives thirty-four verses about the crocodile and ten verses to the glory of the hippo. No wonder G.K. Chesterton wrote "God may be younger than we are!"[1]

He has never grown tired of his world. The elements are created in such a way that each sunset is an original and each snowflake is different. Every baby born is a unique person. God is forever creating and enjoying his creation. The worst thing in the world, says Clyde Kilby commenting on the creative process, is to believe that today is like yesterday.

God notices; he is observant. The Bible says he knows when a sparrow falls. Are you not of more value than they? He keeps on creating in our personal lives, too. He takes all the mistakes, all the broken places and weaves the threads of our lives into something meaningful, as we trust him.

True creativity is always linked up with God. It is part of the adventure to which God calls us. Just living in fellowship with this kind of God is the greatest of creative adventures. As we listen and obey, the Holy Spirit infiltrates into us a likeness to Jesus Christ.

Paul Tournier says, "He calls us to an adventure of faith, difficult and exacting, but full of poetry, of new discoveries, of fresh turns and sudden surprises."

Then why are some of us so small? you ask. Our smallness comes from the desire to "play it safe." Never take any risks. Never make a new decision or trust God in a fresh commitment. We look at our own resources and say, I could never do that. Our scared littleness keeps us in a box.

Adventure or creativity—whichever word you like best—always involves risks. It involves a decision; it is purposive; it is an expression of yourself. Usually it involves others. It stretches you, so that you end up being more than you ever thought you could be. It adds the special flavor to life that makes you feel that you have a secret with God.

At this point you may be thinking of the composition of an exciting piece of music, or a new harmonic arrangement, or a painting, or a poem. And you've already said, "I can't do that." Then don't do that. Find something your own size. It may be learning how to knit; it may be flying a kite on a hillside with your son and getting the tail just the right length so that it will soar out of sight in the blue, blue of the spring sky.

Creativity is taking the stuff of life that exists and shaping it. It is to be for the moment a spark of communication between God and man, reflecting some small piece of his creative nature.

Some of my adventures do not even remotely resemble painting a picture, but they have been big experiences that demanded creativity and resources I didn't know I had. The first wilderness canoe trip into Canada was one of these. My husband and myself in one canoe; our son, Mark and Bill, one of "our boys," in another. An untried river; the equipment and the right amount of food; the skills necessary for survival. When we came to our first cataract (which looked like a giant waterfall to me), I wanted to turn around and go back. Three men let me know firmly that you don't go back on trips like this; we were committed to the river. Often when there seemed no route suitable for portage, I heard my husband say, "Pick up the end of the canoe and follow me."

The black flies ate my husband until he looked measly; the mosquitoes nourished themselves on Bill until he swelled out of shape. It rained; we fought our way through log jams, padled for hours through marsh lowlands. But there were other days. The sun shone, and a whole beautiful world was reflected in the river. No sound, except for the song of the wind in the top of the pines, eighty to a hundred feet tall, and the dip of paddles in the stream. Birds—cedar waxwings, Canada jays, yellow warblers, redstarts. The otter; the moose; the sunset over the lake; the loon's call; the softness of decaying forest underfoot; the splendor of undisturbed wilderness. *Lord, I thought, you made all of this and it was here praising you long before we discovered it. Thank you for sharing it with us.*

That's one kind of adventure. I wouldn't have missed it! But I would never have gone if I hadn't taken the risk, and I might never have gone if I had known the cost in sheer endurance and misery. Think of what I might have missed!

Some people don't have children because they are too busy counting costs, evaluating the risks, and weighing the odds of failure. They will never know what they missed! No one marveling at a child conceived in love, nurtured in the mother, bearing the likeness of both parents can doubt the worth of that kind of creativity.

Excuse me for placing canoe trips and having children in the same category, but I meant to observe that some people are scared of anything that doesn't have a certain end and all the risk removed. No one can really live like that. Life itself is a risk. Yet I am surprised at the number of people who never try anything new. A new recipe. (It may not be good!) A new hairstyle. (I may not like it!) A new game. (I don't know how to play.) A new place. (I've never been there before.)

> *Come weal or come woe*
> *My status is quo.*

We seek a smooth path, without any brambles or stones in the way, a straight way without too much incline that leads us to heaven quite safely. On the other hand, God, the great Adventurer, leads us over high peaks, across rocky crags, up steep ravines, across rivers we thought we couldn't cross, and gets us to heaven all breathless, bearing the fruit of our effort and the likeness of his Son—and fit for royal fellowship.

Eric Berne, author of *Games People Play,* says, "Losers spend their lives thinking about what they're going to do. Winners on the other hand, are not afraid to savor the present, to unpack their books and listen to the birds sing. Losers say *but* and *if only.* Winners are enlightened people who grow rich, healthy, strong, wise and brave using just three words in life: *Yes, No* and *Wow.*"

We need positive attitudes to live creatively. We cannot be encumbered by past failures. The Scripture reaffirms this by urging us to "put off" and "press on." Our sensitive egos may still smart from a risk we took that left us bruised. Bruisings of this kind come most often when the adventures have been our own selfish plans rather than true acts of creativity. But remember God is still the author of new beginnings.

I do not speak lightly of ego needs. For some people telephoning someone else is a great adventure and risk. Introducing someone can be exceedingly painful for others. These are extremes of the spectrum, but they exist. And for such the status is not so much "quo" as human safety. But we are not left to that. An infinitely creative God wants to take us out of our smallness into an adventure suitable for us. We need a positive attitude to begin. We can do it, by his grace.

I'm thinking of such an adventure in my own life. God had brought a woman into my life who was an incipient alcoholic. When life's dreariness or her personal disappointment became too much, she took to the bottle and was out of sight for days.

She became a Christian and her life changed radically, and the community of those who loved her had almost forgotten, if they had even known, about her problem. Then one day a neighbor innocently said something that hit a vulnerable spot in my friend; she was angry and hurt and went home.

The neighbor tried to call, other friends tried to contact her. No answer. Her car sat in the drive, but no one could reach her. On the second day the fear grew that she may have returned to the bottle. It was decided that I was to go to her home. My assignment was a rescue adventure with God, but I was a Jonah at heart. She lived in the country and had two enormous police dogs that usually met the car. I never left my car until she called them off. Would she be there to call them off? I didn't want to go; I was scared; I didn't know what to do once I got there. My husband prayed with me and shoved me out of the house. When I arrived the dogs miraculously weren't outside; I knocked on the door; she answered and fell weeping into my arms, asking, "How do you know if God forgives you?" I was so glad I went!

I did not have a positive attitude toward any detail of the adventure, but I did have a positive attitude toward God, and that is a good place to begin. And I think the illustration points out one other helpful detail; namely, the role of encouraging friends. We can encourage others to take the risk of living creatively.

A positive attitude is inspired by a spirit of thankfulness. One of the most creative exercises a woman can do is to write a weekly theme entitled, "Why I am thankful." Thankfulness changes our negatives to positives, and transforms our liabilities to abilities. A student once wrote a thankful essay for my friend Betty Carlson. It read, "I am thankful for my glasses. It keeps the boys from fighting me and the girls from kissing me."

We need a positive attitude and a spirit of thankfulness, but we also need to uncomplicate our lives. We build stress into our own lives. I'm not suggesting that we leave the sink full of dirty dishes while we enroll in an art class, but we do need to take a careful look at our lives. The details will be different for everyone, but for most it will mean planning ahead to make our lives more orderly and disciplined. There are only twenty-four hours in any one day; make them meaningful as possible. We waste useful energy with self-absorption better spent on being creative.

Except for a few who are able to shut themselves off from the world, our creativity must be flexible, not selfish, and subject to interruption. Particularly is this true of women who have children at home. And if you are truly creative, you will consider even the interruptions creative.

Sometimes our creativity passes through times of darkness when some of our dross is being burned off. You may be in one of those times now as you read this. Nothing has sparkled for you for quite a while. Again, return to faith in a God who sponsors personal adventure and he will help you begin.

What might some of these adventures be? It could be as simple and big an adventure as honesty with a friend. No more role playing, but the risk, the commitment to be who you really are. Real honesty requires integrity. There is a fake kind of honesty popular today that lets people think they have the right to tell a person (with a bit of disguised anger) all the things about that individual that's offensive to them. It's a way of saying, "I don't like lots of things about you, so why don't you do something about it." And it's a neat copout for learning to love. Real honesty might well work on an offensive habit with another person out of love, but it won't make another person unduly responsible for personal hang-ups.

For instance, Sally goes to Anne and says, "I have something against you. I'm jealous of you." What does Anne do? Can she negate everything in herself that makes for the jealousy? No, but Anne can take Sally's false attempt at honesty and make it creative by helping the girl to bear her own burden before God. That's at least a creative response.

The creative risk of adventure in honesty that I first suggested is that of simply letting yourself be known in ways that are free and constructive for you and everyone else. It will undoubtedly include the interchange of letting others help bail you out of your hurts and doing the same for them. A large part of living creatively is reaching outside of your self to help someone else.

Learning to listen helps creative living. Listening may well be second only to loving as a creative act. Listening says so much to the other person about her value. (That's why listening to small children is so important.) But listening lets you hear and know the other person, and you may be surprised at the totally new ideas you encounter.

I read recently of a man who said he had never been bored with anyone. When he began to feel tired of a person, he began to ask, "What is there about the life of this person that makes them so boring?" And by the time he had finished asking questions and listening to them explain themselves he was no longer bored.

The combination of honesty and listening could be a whole new adventure in quality married life for some people. Maybe your husband has never learned how to express himself or share, and you live a lonely existence. If you claim the help of a creative God who designed people with the ability to communicate, and creatively heighten your own sensitivity to your husband, you may be in on one of the biggest adventures of your life. Certainly your prayer life will develop; you'll feel the Holy Spirit controlling your responses; and you will be surprised by more than one miracle.

Never give in to a low quality of life within the home when God, the redeemer, offers his help. One young wife telephoned to say, "Something has been happening to me. It is as if God told me that if I want things to change I am going to have to keep my mouth shut. So I've been trying, and do you know what I've discovered? When you know God you don't always have to be right!"

Another woman has grown beautiful praying for her family and creating an environment that works with her prayers. She prays, "Lord, help my husband not to be so short with Jimmy. He's so sensitive and he never gets a chance to finish what he wants to say. Help John to be more aware of this." And God does.

Making something new and creative out of family life can be a married women's great adventure. It can also be the adventure of the single person, because the close interpersonal relationships within any living situation demand his help.

One of my great adventures as a writer has come from the families who share with me how *Honey for a Child's Heart*[2] has launched them into new adventures as families through sharing of books. Writing a book is an adventure of the riskiest sort. But after the pain and loneliness of the actual production, what joy and reward to see others learn to live creatively because I took the risk of adventure.

Setting up a reading program seems so simple an idea that one hardly thinks of it as creative. And yet books can take us on the finest kind of adventure without ever leaving the house. A good adventure takes discipline, and a well-ordered life is necessary for a reading program. Think of the potential for expanded horizons, for creative thinking, for learning something new!

I was talking about good reading to a group of mission candidates recently and one winsome young man told me later in conversation that he was a poor reader and hardly ever read a book. His story revealed unfortunate situations in first and second grade and a move to a new location in third grade where other students teased him about his inability to read. He developed a barrier against reading. He was bright and his mind retained what he heard, but he didn't like to read. It threatened his view of himself. I asked, "Have you ever asked God to help you overcome this handicap and work on it with divine help?" He thought about it for a minute, and then said, "That would be a choice kind of adventure, wouldn't it?"

Both reading and learning to read fit the category of creative living. My friend may never be a speed reader, and what he sets out to do is easier said than done. But so is painting a picture or playing a musical instrument. It will take courage and sweat and perserverance.

One of my friends declares that learning to change the way you look is a phase of creative living. She says, "God gave you your face; he didn't give you your expression. Why not make it more pleasant?" For others it will be discipline of more sleep, better and less food and a decision to stop chewing the fingernails.

Every meaningful adventure I have had has involved doing something I believed to be the will of God. I have been pushed out over my head in experiences so many times that I've found myself swimming strokes I didn't know I knew! Everything from a radio talk show to taking a chair-lift to the top of the mountain with the intent of skiing down! I was no pro in either event, but I did have some exciting surprises.

I've used the word swimming metaphorically, but it reminds me of a literal swim I once took. Geraldine had just come to trust Christ. We were taking an Exercise and Swim class together at the Y. Following our first day of exercises, we jumped into the pool. She stood there for a minute and said, "I'm, scared to death to put my face in the water, but now that I know God, I'll just say a little prayer and float across the pool on my face." She proceeded to do just that! Leaving me, who had known God for sometime and who always swam with my head well above the water, standing agape. So I said a little prayer and similarly did a prone float across the pool!

The creativity of doing what you believe to be the will of God will more often have significant spiritual dimensions. It may be taking more time with your children, developing a new friendship, helping someone who is needy, or sharing your faith.

Taking seriously the fact that you have been entrusted with the Gospel will bring you your most awesome adventures. Creatively sharing the Good News is a most expanding experience. Every person is unique: they hurt in different places; their capacity for intake of truth varies. To take the great truths of God's redemption and communicate these skillfully takes creativity. We don't dump a load of truth; we interact. We need the right words, the illustrations that apply, the ability to listen—and God's help. No one can ever grow dull or small or uninteresting who grabs hold of this adventure. We have been entrusted with the truth about God!

Living creatively is as big as creation. Don't be among those who think that all birds are sparrows and that there are two kinds of trees; one with leaves and one with needles. Living creatively means noticing, being aware and alive to the world. It involves an appreciation and drive toward excellence. It involves things, people, ideas. God is noticing all the time. Shouldn't we be just a little more awake?

1. Have I recently added any new furniture in my spiritual house?
2. What is my "daily routine" of activities? How often do I willfully alter that routine?
3. Is my creativity often interrupted? How can I make those interruptions a new source for creativity?

Living creatively is an adventure, and all adventures require that we risk something. God is the greatest of painters, poets, plumbers, sculptors and chemists. He "...wants to take us out of our smallness into an adventure suitable for us." Are you ready? Will you take the risk?

The next three chapters focus on our position in the church and our responsibilities to the world. How can we begin to apply our creative riches in our day-to-day world?

When we live creatively, we exercise our talents and our gifts. In the following pages, Jill Briscoe examines the proper heart attitudes of a servant who wants to use her spiritual gifts for the building of Christ's Church. "How are talents different from spiritual gifts?" "What if my church doesn't believe women should teach or preach?" Where would God have me to begin?"

Note: The format of this chapter will be slightly different from the last four. You might try to visualize it as a play with four actors.

OOPS!
I Think I've Discovered
A Gift I Shouldn't Have!

by Jill Briscoe

"I'm the fashion editor for a popular magazine, the vice-president of a home catalog company, mother of six, and chairman of our women's club," said a beautifully groomed modern Prime Rib. "But as far as my church is concerned, all I'm good for is pouring Kool-Aid and cutting up tuna fish sandwiches!"

The Snake rolled over and over with glee. It was true. All those talents and gifts! As long as he provided her with plenty of secular opportunity to exercise them, and as long as the church leadership continued to be so threatened by her and her gifts that they ignored them, all would be well.

The elder from the local assembly, who had been asked to visit said lady in her home and answer her awkward questions, moved uncomfortably from foot to foot.

"Well, they do need help in the nursery," he suggested hopefully.

"I can't stand squelchy, shrieking kids," she said.

"Well, maybe you could help embroider the kneelers for the prayer stools."

"Listen, sir," the lady replied, becoming increasingly frustrated, "that isn't my gift. I know I have the gifts of teaching, administration, and preaching."

"You can't have," replied the man, aghast. "You're not allowed to! God doesn't give such gifts to women!"

"Well, just who do you think I received them from?" she demanded. "The Snake?" She faced him defiantly. "Just where does it say all *that* in the Bible, anyway?"

"In Timothy... Paul says, 'I suffer not a woman to teach,'" answered the man triumphantly.

"Then why did he give instruction for women to cover their heads *when* they were praying and prophesying in public?" inquired the lady tartly.

The Snake was appalled. When had she read *that*? he wondered. He had no idea she had been studying the subject. He usually made sure the Prime Ribs who were gifted by Omnipotence were directed away from such dangerous passages of Scripture. "Keep them in the Martha and Mary bits," he advised his hosts of demons. Also, 1 Peter 3 is good (even though it's really speaking to women married to non-Christians). As they read through their Bibles, throw a dim light on verses like Mark 16:11, where Mary Magdalene tries to teach the disciples that Jesus had risen from the dead, and the Bible says "they believed not!" Tell them men won't believe women teachers because it's not scriptural to listen to them.

Well, the elder left the lady's house shaking his head over all this women's lib stuff. Why she'd refused the offer to teach first graders *and* arrange the flowers, he just couldn't imagine. Just who did she think she was?

After he had gone, the gifted Prime Rib began pacing up and down her living room talking to Omnipotence. Now, that wasn't good at all, the Snake decided. He tried to keep her so angry at the church leadership that she just wouldn't pray. But it didn't work. The whole situation became exceedingly dangerous.

"Omnipotence, am I wrong?" she asked. "Did You gift me to use my talents for the world or for You? I *know* I can speak well. Am I then to spend my life selling cosmetics...or selling Christ?"

Omnipotence was just about to answer when the Snake thought of a neat idea. He *had* to stop her from being turned to Paul's writings! He knew as well as Omnipotence that Paul had lots to say about a woman's gifts and the freedom to exercise such, and he had no intention of letting her get into all that.

"Why don't you start *right at the beginning of your Bible?*" he suggested. "Then work your way through, looking for things to back you up. Surely if God had intended women to be leaders in the church, He wouldn't wait until the New Testament to tell them!"

That made sense to the lady, so she began to read. The Snake curled and knotted his long evil body in black mirth and retired to his bed for a rest. He'd been especially busy the last four hundred years, and he knew it must be safe to take a breather, having directed the lady to the Old Testament. Not that his knowledge of the Old Testament Scriptures was such that he could afford to be complacent. He just knew the women in those times were treated little better than cattle, and even Omnipotence's chosen people, who should have known better, recited a little prayer before the day began. It went something like this: "I thank thee, God, I am not a Gentile, I am not a slave, I am not a woman!" No, the personhood of the Rib had not been vindicated in Old Testament days! He could afford to sleep for a little while.

Omnipotence laughed gently. Sitting down by the lady's side, he turned the pages of her Bible until she arrived at the Book of Exodus, chapter one.

"Let me introduce you to Miriam," He said. "See her standing by the river, having placed her little brother among the crocodiles. Examine her many natural gifts evident in the story: her courage demonstrated by her not running away as the princess appears; her quickmindedness in offering her own mother as nurse to the baby; her clever ability and gift of words as she persuades the princess of Egypt to listen to her *and* follow her suggestions. Here is talent indeed."

"But are talents spiritual gifts?" asked the lady.

"No," replied Omnipotence. "Natural talents are not spiritual gifts. Natural talents are given according to common grace. Many non-believers have natural talents, but no unbeliever has a spiritual gift! These are given by the Holy Spirit when He enters the human heart at conversion. He it is who gifts the believer. Talents have to do with techniques and methods dependent on natural power, and as such are a gift from God. But the Holy Spirit imparts spiritual gifts that enable My children to do not only the natural things better, but supernatural things as well."

"I feel I have some natural talents, Omnipotence," the lady said, quieting down. "I found some of them by exercising and proving them, but how can I learn if I have spiritual gifts? I think I do, but the church will not allow me the opportunity to find out."

"Read on, little lady," replied Omnipotence. "Come with me to Exodus 15 and see Miriam now. She has become a prophetess *in the church!* She is right at the top along with her brothers Moses and Aaron. She is also the choir director. And no one is objecting."

"Oh, if only I could talk to her," said the lady. "If I could ask her how it all happened. Did she have to fight for her rights in a day and age when women were trampled underfoot?"

"It is not altogether a question of rights or roles," said Omnipotence. "It's a question of gifts. Israel recognized her gift. Acknowledging and confirming her spiritual abilities, they held her in the same respect as Aaron and Moses. Her gift led her out of her cultural role, you see.

"I say in My Word," Omnipotence continued, "that the Holy Spirit imparts grace with the gift. The word *grace* means 'charm.' It will be a wonderfully 'charming' thing when you find a way to let the church 'see' in action the gift I have given you. People will be delighted."

"But my church isn't thrilled or delighted."

"You need to take the opportunities they open up to you," counseled Omnipotence. "If all they will allow you to do is teach first grade, then teach first grade. Prove your gift to them. If you have the gift of teaching, you can teach little children as well as adults. Start there with what you are allowed to do. Let your gift become a blessing to the little ones. Then the little ones will tell their parents, and the parents will acknowledge and confirm your charming gift exercised among their precious children. The noise of their approval will break upon the leadership's ears, and they will invite you to 'come up higher.' You have to prove yourself a blessing, not a nuisance! I will do the rest for you. Prime Ribs I placed in the history pages of time, were those who did not demand their rightful place, but allowed Me to place them in My sphere of service."

"But the men in my church seem so threatened," the lady objected. "And I know I don't help. I try to talk about it all, but then we begin to argue, and I get horribly aggressive and domineering!"

"Look at Moses," said Omnipotence. "He was not threatened by Miriam's gifts. But then there was not in all the earth a man as humble as he. Many men need to grow in humility. Under Moses' leadership, Miriam exercised her gift beautifully. She had the ability to prophesy—which means to proclaim a divine message—with results! She declared that which could not be known by natural means. And, oh, how gracefully she did it! What a blessing she became to the whole Israelite nation, and how they loved her—men and women alike."

"Was it always so?" inquired the lady.

"No," replied Omnipotence. "Just once toward the end of her life she usurped Moses' authority—the authority I had invested in him. She chose to rebuke his decision to marry the

Ethiopian woman. Together with Aaron she began to 'fight for her rights,' instead of resting in my position for her. 'Has the Lord spoken by Moses only?' she demanded, 'Has He not also spoken by Aaron and me?' For this I struck from heaven, and she became a leper."

The lady gasped. "So great a punishment, Omnipotence?"

"To usurp Moses' authority was to usurp mine!" returned Omnipotence. "I simply removed her from her position of usefulness and service. She was driven outside the camp in shame. But see, Israel did not travel until she was restored to them again. They needed her, and I needed her. I would not let them journey on without her. But we could do without her pride and arrogance. She had to learn that her God-given talents and gifts must be used freely and to the full *under* the authority I had placed over her. In this case, the man Moses."

"So, there *is* a place for women?" the lady asked hopefully.

Omnipotence laughed. "Read on, little Prime Rib," He said. "Come with Me to Huldah's story."

"Who's she?" asked the lady, who had honestly never heard of her.

"She's another prophetess of Mine," responded Omnipotence. "She lived in the university quarter of the city of Jerusalem in the days of godly King Josiah. She was the lady the priests of My temple and others of My land—Yes, even the king of My country—turned to for advice when they discovered the dusty book of the law in the rubble of My temple. They needed a word of encouragement from God. I sent them to Huldah and gave them a message of hope through her lips."

"Well, that was good," replied the lady, a little doubtfully.

"But what has it to do with our talk?" asked Omnipotence, reading her thoughts. "I'll tell you. Standing by King Josiah's side was Jeremiah the prophet, My 'man of men.' But in that moment of national extremity I sent My people to Huldah, my 'woman of women'! I can speak to a nation through a woman with just as much authority and power as through a man, if I so choose."

"That's where it's at!" the lady almost shouted. "If only I could know it's Your *will* to use me."

"Come to the Gospels," said Omnipotence. "Gabriel invited a woman to make room for My Son in her body. I could just as easily have presented a ready-formed child to a man! A woman was first at My cradle, last at My cross, first at My tomb, and first to be told of My resurrection. They were quicker to believe than My disciples!

"Anna, old and worn, was used to speak for Jesus to all who lived at Jerusalem. What place did women have in My Son's life and ministry and in My kingdom? A large and roomy place."

"But there's still Paul," the lady said.

It was now far into the night. The Snake, sensing all was not well, was awakened from his varied nightmares. To his horror, he saw Omnipotence directing the lady to Paul's epistles.

"No, no!" he shouted. "*Not* Galatians! Try Corinthians and Timothy. Please, please *not* Galatians!"

They ignored him, and Omnipotence read loudly and clearly from Galatians 3:28: "[In Christ] there is neither Jew nor Greek, there is neither bond nor free, there is neither male nor female."

"So," explained Omnipotence, "*all* Paul's commands to those *in Christ* are commands to women as well as men. Why don't we do a study of *those commands* first and measure your obedience, before we take two statements completely out of context and allow the Snake to shut your mouth for the rest of your life?" And so they did.

The Snake was panic-stricken. Hearing Omnipotence's beautiful voice reading the Scriptures was torture enough, but to see the light of liberation dawning in the lady's eyes was worse!

Omnipotence started with a quotation from the Old Testament, one that the Snake had successfully hidden for decades. "The Lord gives the word [of power]; the women who bear and publish (the news) are a great host" (Ps. 68:11, *Amplified Bible*). He then went straight to Romans 10:13-15 and read through it.

> For whosoever shall call upon the name of the Lord shall be saved. How then shall they call on him in whom they have not believed? and how shall they believe in him of whom they have not heard? and how shall they hear without a preacher? And how shall they preach, except they be sent? as it is written, How beautiful are the feet of them that preach the gospel of peace, and bring glad tidings of good things!

Then He turned to 2 Corinthians 5:9, 10:

> Wherefore we labour, that, whether present or absent, we may be accepted of him. For we must all appear before the judgment seat of Christ; that every one may receive the things done in his body, according to that he hath done, whether it be good or bad.

He reminded the lady that she had a primary responsibility to Him. It was He she must stand before to give account of gifts used or abused while on earth.

He took her next to 1 Corinthians 12:28, which says: "And God hath set some in the church, first apostles, secondarily prophets, thirdly teachers, after that miracles, then gifts of healings, helps, governments, diversities of tongues." And He pointed out that if she was a teacher, then He had set her in His body as such, and it was stupid to be used as something else.

Approaching the dreaded verse in 1 Corinthians—14:34—that she had had quoted to her so often, He pointed out that when the men in authority did not permit a woman to speak, she was to be obedient and not to cause dissension. By the same token, if she was commanded to speak, she should also be obedient.

The problem had been partly a cultural thing in the Corinthian church. Paul had actually given great emancipation to New Testament women. Never before had they been allowed to speak in a public gathering. They had not even been allowed to teach their own children at home. Practically none were educated. But *in* Christ, all was changed. Each member of the body of Christ was "sexless" as far as God was concerned. Sex ceased to matter unless a girl had the gift of preaching or teaching, and then it was to be exercised under the authority of the church body. In fact, the leadership's responsibility was to help and enable each member, whatever sex, to discover his or her gift and exercise it under their control, that the whole body might be edified. In Corinth, however, this new freedom had gone straight to some Prime Ribs' heads, and they had leaped the barriers of centuries that commanded, among other things, that women worship in another part of the building and were actually shouting out questions in the worship service. Hence Paul's rebuke, "Let your women keep silence in the churches: for it is not permitted unto them to speak; but they are commanded to be under obedience, as also saith the law. And if they will learn anything, let them ask their husbands at home: for it is a shame for women to speak in the church."

Omnipotence then took the lady to meet Phoebe, a favorite Prime Rib of His. (The Snake had always detested that girl.) Paul listed her among the leaders of the church at Rome, and so she was. The precious letter of Romans that had to be carried hundreds of miles from Corinth to Rome was entrusted to her, a mere woman. This was a job usually given only to specially trained men couriers. (Her courage sickened the Snake.) Her position in the early church was one of patroness or lawyer to the group of believers.

The lady looked long and hard down the list of leaders in Romans 16. Eight were women! Prisca, too, rose from the page of scripture to add her voice to those of Philip's four daughters, all of whom prophesied! Prisca it was who corrected the great Apollos's teaching, his doctrine needing added truth. She supplied it. She and her husband Aquila were apparently dear colaborers with the Apostle Paul.

Then there was Apphia, Philemon's wife. Euodias and Syntyche, teachers there in Philippi, and Lydia, called by Paul, "one who labored by my side."

"Now, put all this beside Paul's strange commandment not to let a woman teach," said Omnipotence. "In Timothy the case was such that the women were usurping the man's authority and therefore needed disciplining. But Paul's encompassing commitment to the gospel forced him generally to give responsibility to the most capable person, regardless of sex."

The study over, Omnipotence closed His book. The lady's eyes were shining, and she thanked Him for directing her to truth that set her free. Free to dedicate her natural talents to her Lord. Free to choose to use her gifts within the church body anywhere they would let her. Free to wait for Omnipotence's time to give her opportunities. And free to start right now with opportunities given and available.

Lifting the phone, she called the elder of her church, who was rather surprised to hear from her.

"I'd like to teach those first graders," she said quietly. The man was glad and grateful. He was tired of trying to draft people into the Lord's service. He was also glad she had found her place. He thanked her and accepted her offer. Putting the phone down, he turned around to find Omnipotence standing there.

"Now it's your turn," Omnipotence said. "Let's get My book out and start examining the whole subject, laying aside all your cultural ideas. And, oh, yes—about the little gifted Prime Rib you've just been talking to. She really can do more than pour your Kool-Aid and cut up your sandwiches! Let's see just how you can help her discover and exercise her gifts, and so edify the body . . . under your leadership, of course."

"But, Omnipotence," he protested, "she thinks she has a speaking gift. She thinks she can preach!"

"She can," Omnipotence replied. "I gifted her. She is one of My gifts to your assembly. Now what are you going to do about it? Accept or reject My gift?"

The lady prayed hard for the elder and for her own attitude as well. Oh, how she longed for Omnipotence to use her. He had promised her he would. She began to dare to believe it would be so! She believed—

Omnipotence could do it,
Omnipotence would do it,
For Omnipotence is Omnipotence,
And Omnipotence is the giver of gifts.

1. *What specific ministry opportunities have I been exposed to lately?*
2. *What service opportunities are available that offer little or no recognition? How would I feel in a non-visible ministry?*
3. *In what ways might I be restricting God's free usage of my gifts and talents?*
4. *If I had my choice of a ministry—any ministry in the church—what would I like to do?*

Not all service will give us visibility in front of our peers. Jesus doesn't ask us to make a big splash, just to do His work. "For everyone who exalts himself will be humbled, and he who humbles himself will be exalted" (Luke 14:11). This is a foundational principle in the Kingdom of God. It is the revolutionary concept which is underscored in the Beatitudes. But we should not abandon our gifts for the sake of humility. Spiritual Gifts must be used if they are to be developed.

Our gifts are developed within the context of a fellowship of believers. As others see the closeness, the honesty and the love exhibited within our group, they will desire to know more about our God. It is not what we do that will facilitate evangelism, but who we are. To the non-believer, the Christian community should be an effective witness of the existence and sufficiency of God.

"How can I get the God-in-me into my non-Christian friends?"

"What happens when I don't live up to my self-expectations?"

The Witness of Community

by Rebecca Manley Pippert

We were not born to be alone. God created us for relationship. So we have been born first into the human family and then as Christians born again into the family of God. All of us, therefore, are members of some kind of community, our own family, school, friends, fraternity, sorority or other social groups. As John Donne has said, "No man is an island."

Still, we often feel like islands. Our professional commitments frequently lead us not only into geographical isolation but emotional isolation as well. And so loneliness—the very opposite of community, the most crushing of all emotions—descends on us. There is an important reason for this. It is by design and not caprice that we find loneliness crushing. Only in community can we become fully alive, fully human, finding rest and completeness in the context of others. It is not enough for one individual to imitate the ways of God. For God is not alone; he is the Trinity. Therefore, it is the community of God's people who will represent him more fully and completely.

Furthermore it is in community—in seeing ourselves juxtaposed with others—that we learn who we are. In community we can exercise the gifts God has given us. In all likelihood these gifts are gifts of ministry. For Christians especially community is glorious. For it is in community that we can worship together, be nurtured and bear one another's burdens.

What, then, is the role of Christian community in evangelism? Some Christians feel that their community (be it a church, a Bible study, a small group or a friendship relationship) can prepare people to be launched out for witness to others. Certainly we need to be fed and nurtured and built up and trained. But we must remember, too, that our local Christian community itself can be a powerful witness to our non-Christian friends. Communities of Christians who practice what they preach arouse and stimulate curiosity in Jesus. When the teaching of Jesus is heard and demonstrated, there will be impact.

No Lone Rangers

We are not called to be "Lone-Ranger" Christians. We are called to love one another. Indeed a legitimate basis for rejection of belief in God, according to Jesus is lack of love among Christians (Jn. 17:20-24). The antihero for Christians is the American cowboy, out there dodging the arrows and bullets alone. Instead we are called to be a close family that welcomes the world into our midst. We invite people to come and share our love and our gifts. We are free to admit we have not arrived and are far from perfect. But because we believe Jesus is the living center of our group, we invite our non-Christian friends and acquaintances to hang around us and observe him.

I used to feel paranoid about the presence of skeptics in Christian groups. Would they feel weird listening to us pray? Watching us read the Bible? When I gave a talk to a group, I used to ask the leaders if there were any nonbelievers present. Upon reflection I realized that even if there were, I would not change my message at all. The world is not as fragile as we think. They can handle us in our natural habitat far more than we realize. All they need is to feel welcome and to be invited to "come and see." In fact, people long to be a part of a community who will care for them (whether it is a Bible study group or a church).

Although that truth is ageless, it has never been more timely than today. For a variety of reasons, people are drawn in more often by the warmth of relationship than the brilliance of apologetics. In fact, people are almost too vulnerable to community; if they feel loved, they will tend to believe anything. This situation is exploited to the fullest by a number of the fringe religious groups like the Unification Church of Sun Myung Moon. As Christians true to Christ we do care about emotional needs, but we must be careful not to manipulate people through it. It is fine that the world is drawn into our midst because they feel welcomed and cared for. But we must be as concerned for their minds as for their souls. We must offer not only love but excellent biblical teaching as well. There has to be solid intellectual content in our warm communities or our houses will be built on shifting sand. The world needs both to feel God's love and hear God's truth in us.

Communities, then, can be powerful tools to communicate the reality of Jesus. Let us take a closer look at some of the forms these communities take.

Christian Bible Study

Our witness as a community can be especially demonstrated through a Bible study group. The group should think of activities to which they could invite their friends. Bruce Erickson, an Inter-Varsity staff member in Oregon, said that his Bible study learned of a man on welfare whose house needed reroofing. Bruce suggested that each member bring a non-Christian friend and make it a "roofing party." Someone would have to be pretty desperate to go to a party like this. But a group spent the day together, working hard, caring for the man and just having fun.

Some of them eventually became Christians. Without realizing it these Christians had been witnessing all day by the way they cared for each other, by their concern for the man, by their ability to have fun! We need to invite people along to see us as we live. Things we take for granted (that we pray for each other, sincerely try to love each other) can make a deep impression.

Another way we can make a lasting impression on the world is in our attitude toward possessions. Jesus talks about few things as much as our possessions. He tells us that no person can serve two masters (Matt. 6:24). To serve God as our first love means there can be no competing loyalties. We can stimulate a curiosity in the gospel when we demonstrate that we believe our money is God's and we desire to use it to please him.

One of the things that grabbed Lois's interest in the gospel was when she came to a fellowship meeting and heard a Christian student say he had no money for a ticket home. Immediately three fellow Christians reached into their pockets and gave what they had. Later when Lois wanted to go to a Christian student conference but had no funds, another Christian told her he would sell his camping tent. He loved camping but felt that her getting nurture for her young faith was more important. When we demonstrate a biblical attitude toward money and material possessions, the world stands up to take notice.

Or take another example. Once a girl told me her Bible study group wanted to reach out to their non-Christian friends, but they could not think of what to do. Then she said quickly that she had to dash to pick up tickets for her group to see *Richard III,* a play she was in. When I told her that would be a great thing for them to take their friends to, she said, "What does *Richard III* have to do with God?"

"For starters, this play deals with the problem of evil. Is Richard responsible for his cruelty or can he blame it on his 'genes' and his crippled body? Any discussion of the nature of evil leads one to discussing ultimate issues," I said.

So here we have an example not only of what to do, but also of the importance of integrating our faith into our world. If we think God is relevant only in Bible studies, our witness will have little impact.

That means we need to be conscious of current political and cultural events. It is not necessary to see or read everything, but we do need to be aware of what our culture is listening to. Then we must develop our analytical skills in evaluating our culture from a Christian perspective. We need a "Christian mind," as Harry Blamires has suggested. I know a woman who does not go to many films. But she reads Pauline Kael's film reviews in the *New Yorker* regularly to gain understanding and awareness of her culture, and it helps her to talk with others. Unfortunately her example is the exception.

When through our Bible studies we reach out to our skeptic friends in love and bring them into our midst, when we live as Jesus would have us live, regarding people as infinitely more important than material things, and when we demonstrate sensitivity and insight rather than ignorance toward our culture, the impact will be great. Our Christian group, then, will not become ingrown and isolated from the surrounding society. Rather we will demonstrate that Christians are real people who care deeply for other people. We study and love the Scripture because it, too, is passionately honest about life and loyal to the truth about us. We meet together as Christians, and we pray and study God's Word because we celebrate the call to live in the real world and are not trying to escape from it.

Nonetheless, perhaps we feel bringing our non-Christian friends to a Bible study full of Christians would be too overpowering at first. We may feel they need something less threatening to start with.

Evangelistic Bible Study

Sooner or later we must get our non-Christian friends reading the Bible. One effective way is to gather several skeptic friends with one or two Christians and study a passage that vitally confronts us with the person of Christ. They need to see Jesus as he walks through Palestine—watch what he does, listen to what he says, observe how he relates to people. This was how his disciples slowly became convinced of who Jesus was. Our friends, too, need to hang around the Jesus in the Gospels.

Many people blindly accept Christ's deity as a child, and then blindly reject it as they grow up, without ever realizing that Jesus comes to us first as a person. Our aim is to allow Jesus to come alive to them in the Scriptures to give them a feel of what kind of person he is.

When you invite your friends, assure them that no previous Bible knowledge is necessary. They do not have to believe in God or the Bible. The point is for them to read firsthand what the Bible actually says. If they do not believe, then for the sake of intellectual integrity they need to know what they are rejecting. We can assure them that it will not be churchy; we will not sing hymns. Rather we will study the passage as we would any historical document, arriving at conclusions that the text, not the teacher, demands.

This is an efficient way to present Jesus. Most people do not recognize their need for Jesus in a one-shot conversation. But when a Christian befriends them and eventually leads them into a study like this, they will grasp a much fuller picture of what it means to be a Christian. Even if we only met six times, we could look at: (1) Jesus' sensitivity and compassion to people (Jn. 4: the woman at the well); (2) his miraculous powers (Jn. 11: Lazarus's resurrection); (3) who he claimed to be (Jn. 14: "I am the way, and the truth, and the life"); (4) how to become a Christian (Jn 3:1-21: Nicodemus); (5) the death of Jesus (Jn.19); (6) his resurrection (Jn. 20).

Most importantly, to lead this kind of study it is not necessary to have lots of experience or training as a Bible study leader. The leader needs to draw out the members as to what the text says, not lecture for an hour.

If you would appreciate help in knowing how to ask the right questions and draw people out, it is not hard to find. Ada Lum has written a very brief but handy guide called *How to Lead an Evangelistic Bible Study* to give sound general help. And she has put together a series of studies on the life of Jesus called *Jesus the Life Changer* which selects key events in the gospels and suggests specific questions you can ask.

The Church

I have said very little about the local church because most of my experience has been within a parachurch organization. It is not that I feel the church is unimportant. On the contrary, all Christians should be involved in a church. Parachurch organizations are not the norm. They will come and go, but the church, the agent of God's action in the world, is for the ages.

Moreover, the church can offer to the world a model that a college Christian group never can. It can offer the model of unity amidst great diversity—diversity of age, race, occupation, ability, interest and so forth. There are inevitable limits to a model of Christ which includes only people who range in age from eighteen to twenty-one.

If you are reading this as a student and you are not associated with a local church, let me say, go immediately and find one where Christ is exalted, the Bible is trusted and acted on, and begin worshiping there. For only there will you find the full scope of what Christian community can mean.

The question is, then, how can churches become communities of faith reaching out and offering life to the world around them? I have often asked pastors how effective their congregations are in reaching out to their local area. Frequently they tell me that their programs are not effective. Many have tried a highly stylized method of evangelism but with meager results. The church members were unaffected, and so was most of the community.

One pastor told me his church spent hundreds of hours training members on exactly what to say as they went door to door sharing the gospel. Three years later, after a tremendous amount of time and effort, only one person who claimed to become a Christian was still walking with God. He said the reason was that the Christian who came to his door cultivated a genuine friendship with him and invited him to meet his network of Christian friends.

The pastor was so struck by that that his congregation began focusing on building strong small group neighborhood Bible studies. He provided Bible study and small group training and encouraged them to reach out to their non-Christian neighbors. For the first time the members of his church began to trust each other, love each other and become truly involved in each other's lives. Then when they formed friendships with non-Christians in their neighborhood, they genuinely wanted them to meet their friends in the Bible study. Soon the Bible study members were bringing their non-Christian friends to their group and eventually their church. The pastor told me that for the first time during his ministry there, real evangelism was going on in his church.

There is a reason for this. Using structures like door-to-door knocking or tracts or a prepared speech is not necessarily wrong, but such methods have limits. They may be useful to a person who has never opened his or her mouth about God and who needs something to start the ball rolling. We all have to start somewhere, and if we feel that a certain method helps us initiate a conversation, then so be it. The ultimate aim, of course, is for our evangelism to flow naturally from our lives and thus reflect a style that is truly consistent with who we are. But no one arrives at that destination all at once. It may take lots of practice, false starts and perhaps even mechanical beginnings before we feel at ease in witnessing.

There are, however, limits to using techniques to talk to a person about Christ. Door-to-door knocking may help get a hearing, but once you are inside the door, your orientation can never be the same again. You only meet a stranger once. From that first meeting some kind of relationship will follow.

It is the same with surveys—asking a person a set of questions designed to draw out their interest in spiritual matters. They may be helpful the first time you talk to a person. But you can only use a survey once. The next time you see that person you cannot whip out the same survey or use another opening technique. The closer you become to an individual, the more awkward you will feel using such methods.

Most "contact" evangelism techniques are severely limited by the fact that nonbelievers never see the gospel fleshed out in the believer's life. One of the greatest gifts (and evidence) that we give is the chance to see how Jesus lives his life through us. And the demonstration of his love, his holiness and his charity is far more powerful in a community of believers than in any individual. Strangers, so long as they remain strangers, only hear a message and never see it lived out in human relationships.

Another limit to contact evangelism is that the very style itself is usually associated with salesmanship. Jesus thus appears simply as another product on the religious market.

Moreover, since this is used by so many fringe religious groups, non-Christians often ask, "Now which one are you? Are you into Hare Krishna, the Moonies, Scientology or what?"

We are then reduced to saying, "No, I'm into the Jesus thing." And so we become one option among thousands because our initial approach has been like all the others. We live in a culture of people who feel like burned over ground. They have heard it all. They have been assaulted by every trip imaginable. And when our style or initial approach reminds them of all the others, Jesus is reduced in their estimation to merely one option among many.

I am not saying there is no place for contact evangelism. But I am saying that by far the most effective, the most costly and even perhaps the most biblical kind of evangelism is found in the person or groups who look at the people around them, those with whom their own life naturally intersects and then begin to cultivate friendships and to love them. When churches start to reach out to their neighborhoods through small groups, the impact can be overwhelming.

Freedom to Fail

We can learn a great deal of information, be full of zeal, master conversational skills, walk closely with God, participate in his community on earth and still blow it. That is one reason God told us so many stories of individuals in the Bible. He knew we would need the encouragement!

Take Peter. He loved Christ, and yet he constantly made mistakes. His most grievous error came in the last moments of Jesus' life. Jesus had told Peter he would deny knowing him, but Peter staunchly rejected the idea. After Jesus was arrested, Peter denied three times ever knowing him. He even invoked a curse upon himself if he knew him. As the cock crowed, what Jesus said had come to pass, Peter had denied the Lord.

Imagine how desolate Peter felt after Jesus' death. The last contact Peter had with Jesus was the scene of his own betrayal. In Jesus' most difficult moment when he needed support the most, Peter had turned against him. Then a few days later Peter was told that the Lord has risen. Jesus was alive; his friends had actually seen him.

How did Peter feel now? He probably had ambivalent feelings. On one level he would be ecstatic, but on another afraid and ashamed. Maybe the Lord had given up on him. Maybe Jesus would feel Peter had made one too many mistakes.

But God knew how Peter felt. He had a messenger tell the women who first came to the tomb, "Go tell his disciples and Peter" that he had risen (Mk. 16:7). "And Peter"—two of the most beautiful words in the Bible. So the disciples went and said, "Guess what? Jesus has risen! A messenger from God told us to go and tell you he's here. Peter, he said to tell you especially!" Only two words, but they brought a world of hope to a man.

And what did Jesus say to Peter when he saw him (Jn. 21:15-17)? He asked, "Peter, do you love me?"

And Peter said, "Yes, Lord, I do."

And so Jesus asked again, "Peter, do you love me?"

Peter perhaps hesitated a bit, and then said, "Yes, Lord, you know I love you."

And then Jesus asked the third time, reminding Peter only too well of his recent painful history of thrice rejecting Jesus.

"And Peter was grieved" and he said, "Lord, you know everything; you know that I love you."

Peter realized that Jesus knew who he was, his fallibility, his limits, his warts. And yet Peter loved Jesus. Jesus knew that too. He had known Peter's faults long before they ever dawned on Peter. And Jesus told him, "Feed my sheep."

Earlier Jesus had nicknamed Peter (Mt. 16:18). Of all the names to choose, Jesus picked the least likely: he called him Rock. We might have selected another, like Shifty or Quivery or To-and-Fro or Sandy. But Jesus chose Rock.

Jesus is telling us something through this. First of all, he knows us—me, you. He knows your limits, your broken promises, your failures. But he also knows that beneath all of that, you have a heart of love for him. He knows that you care. And Jesus also has a name for you, a name you would have never picked for yourself, or dared to dream. He sees what he is making you into; he knows what he has in store for you. And he gives you a name that suits what you are going to become.

We are people of hope and not despair because we have a future that has been secured by God.

More important than our wobbly love for him is his absolute unswerving love for us. When Peter told Jesus he would always remain faithful to him, Jesus knew his resolve would crumble. Nonetheless, he said, "Simon, Simon, behold, Satan demanded to have you, that he might sift you like wheat, but I have prayed for you that your faith may not fail" (Lk. 22:31). And he went on to say, "When you have turned again, strengthen your brethren." Our Lord would not let Peter go. His love is the absolute of the universe.

Jesus knows our warts, but he also knows we love him. He knows what we will look like someday, not a grain of sand as we so often feel, but a beautiful rock, and he loves us, eternally and mightily. And so he turns to us, as he did to Peter, and says, "Feed my sheep." It is that simple. Whatever gifts you have been given, whatever likes or talents, use them, give them, spend yourself on God's world as Jesus spent himself on you. Comfort his people.

Paul prayed as he wrote to the church in Corinth, "Blessed be the God. . . of all comfort, who comforts us in all our affliction, so that we may be able to comfort those who are in any affliction, with the comfort with which we ourselves are comforted by God" (2 Cor. 1:3-4). Earl Palmer says that the word *comfort* in this passage is most accurately described like this: a person is walking down a road alone and he is then joined by another who walks alongside so he does not have to walk the rest of the road alone. And so we might retranslate the text this way: "Blessed be the God who has walked alongside of us, who walked alongside of us in our affliction, so that we may be able to walk alongside of others in their affliction with all of the 'walking-alongsidedness' which we have experienced."

That is what God is like—he is the One who walks alongside. And that is what he calls his children to do. Regardless of age, temperament, fears, inhibitions, he bids us to feed his sheep.

What will we look like? We will look like a man I have only heard about. When I first came to Portland, Oregon, I met a student on one of the campuses where I worked. He was brilliant and looked like he was always pondering the esoteric. His hair was always mussy, and in the entire time I knew him, I never once saw him wear a pair of shoes. Rain, sleet or snow, Bill was always barefoot. While he was attending college he had become a Christian. At this time a well-dressed, middle-class church across the street from the campus wanted to develop more of a ministry to the students. They were not sure how to go about it, but they tried to make them feel welcome. One day Bill decided to worship there. He walked into this church, wearing his blue jeans, tee shirt and of course no shoes. People looked a bit uncomfortable, but no one said anything. So Bill began walking down the aisle looking for a seat. The church was quite crowded that Sunday, so as he got down to the front pew and realized that there were no seats, he just squatted on the carpet—perfectly acceptable behavior at a college fellowship, but perhaps unnerving for a church congregation. The tension in the air became so thick one could slice it.

Suddenly an elderly man began walking down the aisle toward the boy. Was he going to scold Bill? My friends who saw him approaching said they thought, "You can't blame him. He'd never guess Bill is a Christian. And his world is too distant from Bill's to understand. You can't blame him for what he's going to do."

As the man kept walking slowly down the aisle, the church became utterly silent, all eyes were focused on him, you could not hear anyone breathe. When the man reached Bill, with some difficulty he lowered himself and sat down next to him on the carpet. He and Bill worshipped together on the floor that Sunday. I was told there was not a dry eye in the congregation.

The irony is that probably the only one who failed to see how great the giving had been that Sunday was Bill. But grace is always that way. It gives without the receiver realizing how great the gift really is.

As this man walked alongside of his brother and loved him with all that he had received from Christ's love, so must we. This man was the Good Samaritan. He made Bill feel welcome, feel as if he had a home. So he also knew the secret of the parable of the Prodigal Son: there finally is a homecoming because we really have a home to come to.

1. What groups do I belong to that automatically exclude others? What am I doing to include those who are left out?
2. In what ways have I applied the teachings which I receive at church? The teachings which I receive in Bible studies or share groups? Where can I begin?
3. Who are some non-Christian friends that I could invite to an informal Bible study?
4. How do I feel when I fail? How long does it take me to recover?

"Only in community can we become fully alive, fully human, finding rest and completeness in the context of others," Rebecca Pippert writes. Those outside the community of Christ look to us to discover the reality, character and sufficiency of our God. If they do not see God incarnated in Christians and Christian fellowship, they probably will not see Him at all. But we cannot put on Christian community as if it were a garment. It must be a natural emanation of who we are within, as individuals and corporately. Only then will the God-in-me be recognized for what it is—the living God indwelling the spirit of His child.

Part of the Spirit's ministry in us and through us is that of encouragement. The Holy Spirit encourages us by reminding us of God's truth (John 16:13), through the Word of God. We cannot encourage others unless we have a solid base. In the following chapter, Gene A. Getz tells us what that base is, and how we can develop it in our experience.

"Am I a people-encourager?"

Encourage One Another
by Gene A. Getz

"Therefore *encourage one another* and build each other up"
(1 Thessalonians 5:11)

    The Apostle Paul had one important concern that was constantly on his mind and heart—to do all he could when he could to build up the body of Christ. And knowing he could only do so much as an individual, his strategy was to transfer this concern to others—to encourage *every other Christian* to develop the same concern for *all other Christians* (Col. 2:2; 4:8).
    Paul's concern, of course, forms the basic purpose of this book: to provide believers with biblical and practical guidelines for developing a functioning church. In short, to help Christians build up and edify one another.
    As with Paul in the first century, no one Christian in the 20th Century can build up all other believers in a local church. God's design and plan is that *every Christian* be a functioning part of the body of Christ; that every Christian contribute to the process. "The whole body," wrote Paul, must be "joined and held together by *every* supporting ligament." And as the body draws strength and direction from its Head, Jesus Christ, it then "grows and builds itself up in love, as each part does its work" (Eph. 4:15-16).
    Paul's directive to the Thessalonian Christians, near the end of his first letter to this dynamic New Testament church, is

an appropriate exhortation with which to conclude our study. "Therefore, encourage one another and *build each other up.*" And then he added, "just as in fact you are doing" (1 Thes. 5:11).

Here was a "functioning" church. Though they were facing severe trials and persecutions (1 Thes.1:6), and though they were yet to face the trauma of doctrinal disturbance (2 Thes. 2:1-4), Paul commended them for their concern and love for one another. They had learned the importance of mutual encouragement, exhortation, and comfort. Thus Paul commended them, but encouraged them to continue.

The basic Greek word, *parakaleo,* used in 1 Thes. 5:11, appears in several forms in the New Testament. At times the word is translated "to exhort, to admonish, or to teach", at other times, "to beg, entreat, or beseech." It is also translated "to console; to encourage; to comfort."

But the basic word is always used for one primary purpose—to describe functions that will help Christians to be built up in Christ, or to help them to build up one another in Christ. It is the latter meaning that is in mind in this final chapter. And it is this meaning that Paul had in mind when he exhorted the Thessalonian Christians to "encourage one another and build each other up."

The Primary Means for Encouraging One Another

Paul particularly made it apparent what constituted the primary means for mutual encouragement—God's truth! This is why he wrote to the Ephesian Christians, encouraging them to continue "speaking the truth in love." Then he said, "we will in all things grow up into Him who is the Head, that is Christ" (Eph. 4:15).

Many biblical examples demonstrate that the primary means for encouraging other believers focuses in God's truth. For example, Paul, giving the qualities for eldership in his letter to Titus, emphasized that a pastoral leader "must hold firmly to the *trustworthy message* as it has been taught, so that he can *encourage others by sound doctrine* and refute those who oppose it" (Titus 1:9).

When he wrote to Timothy, he charged this young minister: *"Preach the Word;* be prepared in season and out of season; correct, rebuke and *encourage*—with great patience and careful instruction" (2 Tim. 4:2). Furthermore, when Paul, Silas, and Timothy discipled the new Christians at Thessalonica, they dealt with each one of them, just as a "father deals with his own children, *encouraging, comforting,* and *urging* [them] to live lives worthy of God" (1 Thes. 2:11-12).

Paul went on to make clear what the means was for encouraging them to live lives worthy of God: "We also thank God continually because, when you received the *Word of God,* which you heard from us, you accepted it not as the word of men, but as it actually is, the *Word of God,* which *is* at work in you who believe" (1 Thes. 2:13).

The Thessalonian Example

The Christians in Thessalonica illustrate the process of mutual encouragement by means of God's Word probably more significantly than any other New Testament church. Let's look at the specific ways in which this encouragement is demonstrated.

1. The truths regarding the "dead in Christ"

Even though Paul had instructed the Thessalonian Christians specifically regarding the second coming of Christ (2 Thes. 2:5), they were still confused about those who had died. Somehow they got the impression that those who had passed away may not go to be with the Lord when He comes again. Thus Paul wrote to clarify the issue: "Brothers, we do not want you to be ignorant about those who sleep, or to grieve like the rest of men, who have no hope. We believe the Jesus died and rose again and so we believe that God will bring with Jesus those who sleep in Him" (1 Thes. 4:13-14).

Paul went on to explain thoroughly how this would happen: "The dead in Christ will rise first. After that, we who are still alive and are left will be caught up with them in the clouds to meet the Lord in the air. And so we will be with the Lord forever" (1 Thes. 4:16-17).

And then Paul added this very important exhortation—"Therefore, *encourage each other with these words*" (4:18). In other words, build one another up with this marvelous truth. Remind each other of God's promises. Comfort one another with the fact that *all* believers will spend eternity with Jesus Christ, even though they may die before He comes again. Use God's truth to provide one another with assurance and security.

This, of course, was important to these believers. Some of them—along with New Testament believers elsewhere—actually faced the threat of death because of their faith. How frustrating it must have been to be waiting for Christ's return, not knowing that if they were killed or died naturally before He returned, that they would go to be with Christ just as those who were still alive.

2. *The truth regarding the Rapture of the church*

The Thessalonians had yet another problem. They knew that the day of the Lord—the day of judgment and wrath—was coming upon the earth. And they knew it would "come like a thief in the night" (1 Thes. 5:2). But they evidently did not know what would happen to them before this great and terrible time would come. Thus Paul proceeded to clarify God's truth about the matter. With great assurance in his own heart he wrote: "For God did not appoint us to suffer wrath but to receive salvation through our Lord Jesus Christ. He died for us so that, whether we are awake or asleep, we may live together with Him" (1 Thes. 5:9-10). And then he added another significant exhortation: "Therefore, *encourage one another* and build each other up" (5:11).

Here again Paul encouraged them with God's divine perspective—with God's truth. Then he directed them to *"en-*

courage one another" with this same truth.

It was this truth that would help build up the body of Christ at Thessalonica. It was this truth that would provide them with stability and assurance as they faced their present trials and the uncertainty of their immediate future. And it was this kind of truth that would enable them to "become mature, attaining the full measure of perfection found in Christ" (Eph. 4:13). And it was no doubt this kind of truth that Paul was referring to when he wrote to the Ephesians: "Then we will no longer be infants, tossed back and forth by the waves, and blown here and there by every wind of teaching and by the cunning and craftiness of men in their deceitful scheming" (Eph. 4:14). In other words, false teaching creates instability and insecurity. God's Word leads to maturity.

3. *The truth regarding the day of the Lord*

The Thessalonian Christians were very vulnerable in the area of eschatology. Satan made this doctrine a key point of attack in their lives. After Paul wrote his first letter, reassuring them regarding the dead in Christ and the rapture of the church that would deliver them from the wrath of God, a false teacher unsettled them, teaching them that "the day of the Lord" had already come (2 Thes. 2:2). Paul immediately wrote a second letter, reassuring them that the day of the Lord had *not* come. He reminded them of their conversion experience—that God had chosen them "to be saved through the sanctifying work of the Spirit and through *belief in the truth.*" God had called them to "share in the glory of our Lord Jesus Christ"—that is, in His coming (2:13-14).

Paul ended his exposition of God's perspective on the matter with a rather familiar ring in his Thessalonian epistle: "So then, brothers, *stand firm* and *hold to the teachings* we passed on to you, whether by word of mouth or by letter. May our Lord Jesus Christ Himself and God our Father, who loved us and by His grace gave us *eternal encouragement* and good hope, *encourage and strengthen* you in every good deed and word" (2:15-17).

Here again we see Paul using God's truth to encourage the Thessalonians. Interestingly, he refers to *"eternal* encouragement." This, of course, is what makes God's Word so powerful, so significant, so reassuring. We are not sharing human philosophy or temporal concepts and ideas that are limited to space and time. Rather, Jesus said, "Heaven and earth will pass away, but My words will never pass away" (Matt. 24:35). This is why God's Word is to be the primary means Christians are to use to "encourage one another" and "to build one another up."

Practical Steps for Helping Christians Encourage One Another
Step 1

All Christians must realize how important the Word of God is in building up others within the body of Christ. And all Christians must be challenged to learn what God's Word says. They must be ready to share the Word with others who are in special need of encouragement. In other words, Christians cannot mutually encourage one another with Scripture if they are not familiar with Scripture. Therefore, encourage each believer in your church to study the Word of God—not only for personal growth, but to be able to assist others in their growth.

Step 2

Evaluate your church structure in view of this New Testament exhortation. Many traditional churches are designed not for "body function" but for "preacher function." Only the pastor or minister or some other teacher is delegated to share the Word of God with others in the church. Some pastors insist on being the only interpreter of Scripture in the church. The Bible teaches that every Christian must be involved in this process. All Christians are to "speak the truth in love."

Don't misunderstand! It is not wrong for a pastor or teacher to open the Word of God through an extended exposition and message. In fact, this is good, right, and necessary. It was one means in the New Testament for teaching and preaching. But it was not the only means. In fact, more emphasis is placed in Scripture on mutual and informal teaching than on individual and formal communication. This probably is what the author of the Hebrew letter had in mind when he wrote "Let us consider how we may spur *one another* on toward love and good deeds. Let us not give up meeting *together,* as some are in the habit of doing, but let us *encourage one another*—and all the more as you see the Day approaching" (Heb. 10:24-25).

Christians in New Testament days met together for the body of Christ to function—to mutually encourage each other. Though there was certainly formal teaching, there was also informal teaching. This is why Paul wrote to the Colossians, "Let the *Word of Christ* dwell in you richly as you *teach and counsel one another* with all wisdom" (Col. 3:16).

In many of our 20th-century churches, we need to reevaluate our church structures in the light of New Testament principles and exhortations. Many patterns and approaches are so tightly structured that only what is planned can happen. This stifles the creative ministry of the Holy Spirit. It also causes many Christians to become very dependent on a pastor or, at the most, on leaders to take the responsibility for encouragement and exhortation.

What about your church? What are the patterns like? Is there freedom for every member of the body of Christ to function—"to encourage one another" and "to build one another up"?

Moving from Principles to Patterns

As I conclude this chapter I'd like to share a personal experience. Several years ago, after being a professor for nearly 20 years, first at the Moody Bible Institute and later at Dallas Theological Seminary, I helped start a new church in Dallas,

Texas. I'd been studying the New Testament church for several years prior to that time. In fact, I had written a book entitled *Sharpening the Focus of the Church*—a study of New Testament church principles. Several Christians in Dallas heard that I had written the book and that it was in the process of being published. They asked me to share these principles in a small home meeting. I did. Among the principles I shared was the importance of "body function" as embodied in the "one another" concepts which I have developed at length in this present volume.

What happened as a result of that meeting somewhat surprised me. That very evening they wanted to start a church—a church that would build structures and patterns upon what we believed were New Testament principles. One of those principles was that there is no such thing as an absolute form or pattern for the church. Rather, God gives us principles to guide us. He then sets us free to develop structures that are relevant to a particular culture at any given moment in history.

To make a rather long story short, let me quickly bring you up to date on what has happened. We did start a church. We did develop creative forms. My plan at the time was to just help start it—and then to continue my full-time teaching ministry at the seminary. But God had other plans—for me particularly. We immediately experienced a minor explosion in interest and growth. And today—four years after the publication of *Sharpening the Focus of the Church*, we now have four separate congregations that meet in one building. We have also started three branch churches in the Dallas area. We are planning for several more. Our full-time staff for the four churches which meet in one building now totals eight. We purchased an existing building which seats 300 people. We have built two additional buildings for cash—one which houses our Learning Center for children and another to serve as an office complex for our staff. Because we are now making multiple use of the buildings and investing our money primarily in people, rather than in additional buildings, we are now able—as of this writing—to give 25% of our gross receipts to missions. Hopefully we'll be able to reach 50% in the next couple of years.

In a sense, all that I have described is form. You cannot find it in the New Testament. It is cultural. But we believe it's built upon biblical functions and principles. What we have done represents freedom to be what God wants us to be in the light of New Testament principles. At the heart of these principles stand the "one another" concepts—the concepts developed in this book. Yes, we have formal teaching, but we also have time scheduled for the body of Christ to function—to build itself up.

Let me conclude by illustrating how this can work. In our situation each congregation meets once a week for two and half hours. (We now have a Friday night congregation, a Sunday morning congregation, a Sunday afternoon congregation, and a Sunday evening congregation. And we are planning a Saturday night congregation.) Our first hour usually is a formal teaching period—formal in the sense that someone opens the Word of God for an extensive period of time. The second hour, following a coffee break in which we fellowship together, is what we call a fellowship and sharing service. Led by one of our elders or pastors, anyone in the church is permitted to participate—by sharing personal prayer needs, by sharing answers to prayer, by sharing Scripture, by requesting songs, by sharing special music (which is usually planned ahead of time), etc. The results have been exciting. And the ministry to one another is very edifying. In fact, as a full-time pastor (I still teach part-time at Dallas Theological Seminary) I usually sit through four different sharing services each weekend, but never grow tired of the experience. My life is constantly edified by other members of the body of Christ.

Let me explain with this final illustration: In one of the churches I noticed a man walk in who had not been present for many months. I knew he was having a moral problem. I was probably the only one present who paid particular attention to his being there and one of the very few who knew he had a problem. As a body, we "happened" to be sharing Scripture with one another. To my amazement, one after another, people stood up and shared Scripture that had a direct bearing on this man's problem. Those who shared, of course, knew nothing of this man's situation. But the Holy Spirit did—and on one of those rare occasions, I was allowed to see God at work in a dramatic way through various members of Christ's body.

I firmly believe that this kind of experience should not be a rare one. Rather, our 20th-century churches should be structured so that it can happen regularly. And if we will only study the principles of Scripture and develop patterns that are biblically and culturally related, I believe God will do great things through His people.

If you were to ask me why this work has grown and expanded so rapidly, I would not be able to give you a simple answer. One thing I'm sure of however: It's been a result of many factors—both human and divine. A study of history has taught me that no one man can take credit for God's doing.

One thing stands out as being very important in this ministry—the "body of Christ." *Every member* contributes to its success. It has been a corporate effort by a group of people who believe the Bible, who believe in the God of the Bible, who love and care for "one another," and who want all men to be saved and to experience fellowship with God and with other believers. This is a dynamic that God has promised to bless. This dynamic is what Jesus prayed for when He was yet on earth. And with that prayer I conclude: "My prayer is not for them alone. I pray also for those who will believe in Me through their message, that all of them may be one, Father, just as You are in Me and I am in You. May they also be in Us so that the world may believe that You have sent

Me. I have given them the glory that You gave Me, that they may be one as We are one: I in them and You in Me. May they be brought to complete unity to let the world know that You sent Me and have loved them even as You have loved me" (John 17:20-23).

1. What Scriptures do I know that I can use effectively to encourage others? What verses have helped me recently? Name three.
a.
b.
c.
2. How can I be an encourager within our present church structure? What changes might make it easier for our local body to encourage one another?
3. What can I do to help others contribute to the building of Christ's church?
a.
b.
c.

The Bible exhorts us to encourage each other, to build up one another, to inspire each other with God's truth. When we use the Word of God to strengthen others, we tap into the eternal source of stability, hope and joy. Our own words bring only temporary comfort. Still, we must remember that "no one Christian can build up all other believers in the local church." But we can begin with ourselves, encouraging others to be encouragers. We must make time to share Scripture with our Christian friends, both with individuals and with the body of believers.

We have now completed the first two sections of this book. As we move on into the third section, we need to change our focus. In the first four chapters we looked at our self-image from a Biblical perspective. Then we read three chapters which focused on our position in the church and our responsibilities in the world. The next three chapters examine the employment of our God-given spiritual gifts.

"What is my spiritual gift?—Do I really have one?"

"How would God develop this ability for the building up of His church?"

The Ministering Woman Employs Her Gifts

by Pamela Heim

Picture yourself wrapped in festive paper and tied with a fancy bow. Then imagine God's handing the beribboned you to your church; to your neighborhood schools, hospitals, nursing homes; to your community or family. This is not a farfetched idea. You are God's special blessing to your world. He has given you a spiritual gift so that you may be a gift to those around you.

What is a Spiritual Gift?

What is a spiritual gift? It is an ability God gives to every believer in order to serve Him and His church. "Now concerning spiritual gifts. . . I do not want you to be unaware . . . to each one is given the manifestation of the spirit for the common good."[1] "Each one . . ." You, as a child of God, are a gifted person. We hear talk of a gifted child or a gifted speaker or a gifted performer as if giftedness were some rare quality. In the church of Jesus Christ, giftedness is not unusual; it's the norm. No Christian can legitimately say, "I have no gifts. There's no service I can perform in the work of the church." The Bible states otherwise.

This matter of giftedness includes both sexes. Paul reminds

us, "There is neither male nor female; for you are all one in Christ Jesus."[2] The tragedy of our day is not that women constitute over half of church membership. The disaster is that 50 percent are not encouraged to release their tremendous spiritual dynamic. One writer called this stifling of women's gifts a form of blasphemy against the Holy Spirit.[3] Women have spiritual gifts and are responsible before the Lord for discovering, developing and using them. For further light on the subject, study again the account of the talents recorded in Matthew 25:14-30.

Recognizing your giftedness is not pride. To refuse to admit your Spirit-given abilities is dishonest, not humble. I have blonde hair. I like having blonde hair. I did not do a thing to obtain my coloring; my genes determined that for me. If I were to state I did not have blonde hair, I would prove my stupidity, not my modesty. So it is with spiritual gifts. Disclaimers only reveal one's ignorance, not one's humility.

All this is not to say one cannot become puffed up from focusing on her God-given ability. Every good gift from the Lord can be perverted. However, it need not be and should not be abused. Self-importance is checked by the realization that the gifts are given, not attained.

"But one and the same Spirit works in all these things, distributing to each one individually just as He wills."[4] Not as you or I will. Not according to goodness or spiritual maturity. We cannot work to achieve gifts. We do not receive them as rewards for meritorious service. Meritorious service is the result of effectively doing what the Holy Spirit has equipped us to do. That brings us to the importance of knowing one's spiritual gifts.

Knowing One's Gifts

Unused gifts waste the grace of God and choke spiritual life both personally and corporately. To denigrate the importance of recognizing and using one's gifts is to call for the deletion of significant portions of the Bible and to reject God's plan for the building up of His Body. The emphasis of Romans 12, 1 Corinthians 12-14 and Ephesians 4 is that the gifts insure the correct functioning of the church. Christ promised to build His Church[5] and He has given gifts to that end. If our churches and more particularly our women's ministries flounder, we do well to examine the extent to which we encourage the identification and operation of gifts.

A woman may be sincere, dedicated and eager to serve the Lord but fail miserably if placed in a job which she simply cannot do. Too often the church takes any warm, willing body, stuffs it into a vacant slot and expects God to somehow bless the effort. As a "Peanuts" cartoon once pointed out: "sincerity doesn't win ballgames." It doesn't guarantee successful service either. Spirit-filled women using their Spirit-given abilities ensure effective ministry.

Both the church and the individual suffer when one's gifts are not identified. In the last chapter we mentioned that self-esteem grows by realizing that God has handpicked gifts and unique ministry for each of us. As Leslie Flynn puts it, "For every gift He bestows, the Spirit has planned a sphere of service. Thus, no child of God should have an inferiority complex. Rather, an awareness that he is a gifted child with an area of ministry should meet every child of God's psychological need to feel wanted and to possess a sense of worth."[6]

A Sense of Worth and Purpose

The knowledge that I am a gifted person with specific functions I can perform gives me a sense of worth and purpose as nothing else does. Today I am using my teaching gift through my writing ability. Tomorrow I plan to use my teaching gift in a small Bible study group. Today I've been working hard but I feel invigorated, enthusiastic, positive about myself and my part in the Body. Because of past experience, I expect to feel the same way tomorrow. Nothing brings me a greater sense of joy and fulfillment than doing what God has equipped me to do.

I have also served in areas where I've not been gifted. I've been in charge of lining up refreshments for children's vacation Bible school. I've done door-to-door evangelism. I've cleaned the church building. I've sewed for missionaries and rolled bandages. In some of these jobs, I've performed satisfactorily and was satisfied that I had indeed done what had to be done. In others, I've failed and felt frustrated.

If my service to God were solely in those areas where I'm not gifted, I would likely become *very* weary in well-doing. However, interspersed with cooking lunch for our church's innercity preschool and helping with book karate at my children's school are opportunities to teach the Word through writing and speaking. It's the latter ministry that gives zest and promotes growth in my life.

Can you fill a role without having a gift? Can you be a teacher without having the teaching gift? Yes. Should you be a witness without having the gift of evangelism? Certainly. Can you take a meal to a new neighbor without having the gift of helps/service? Of course. More basically, can you be using a gift you don't recognize having? Undoubtedly. But for sheer delight in ministry, knowing and using your spiritual gifts can't be beat. "The delight a person finds in ministering his gift is subconsciously communicated to the recipients of his ministry. The overflow of delight reinforces the exercise of a gift."[7]

Knowing your spiritual gift(s) is basic to knowing God's will, according to Peter Wagner. Commenting on Romans 12:1-9, he says, "To do the 'good and acceptable and perfect will of God' you must think soberly of yourself. To think soberly you must be realistic about your measure of faith. Your measure of spiritual faith is the spiritual gift that has determined which member of the Body you are and what is the special task God has given you to perform for the rest of your life."[8]

Or as Elizabeth O'Connor put it, "We ask to know the will of God without guessing that his will is written into our very beings. We perceive that will when we discern our gifts."[9] I would guess that if you asked Christian women if they wanted to fulfill God's plan for their lives most would say, "Yes." Yet I doubt that any significant number of those could positively tell you what their gifts are.

Using Your Gifts

How then does the average church woman get involved in ministry? My observations lead me to believe:

1) Some women perform ministries because they haven't learned how to say no—whether from weakness or other reasons.

2) Others do church work because of coercion through guilt, fear of social pressure. Some leaders play these folks like a piano: "After all God has done for you, how can you refuse to do this." "If this work fails, God will hold *you* accountable." "Jane has three preschool children also, but *she* still finds time to help." God, forgive us such tactics!

3) Some women labor in the church because they see a need and do something about it. They work in an area in which they are not gifted; this is essential in most churches. Last week I said I would not act as a greeter in my church. I could refuse because a) my church has many potential greeters among its 4,000 members and b) my husband and I are already busy giving leadership to our 500 member Sunday school class. In a small church, I probably would consent to be greeter, pianist, Sunday school teacher and anything else time and energy would permit—making sure my primary thrust was in the areas of my gifts.

4) Then there are those blessed women whose gifts are recognized and put to use. May their tribe increase! And may God grant us the wisdom to make it happen. When it doesn't, the church reminds us of the following story.

Once upon a time (as all good stories begin), twenty people with Ph.D.'s decided to set up their own university. They believed they had something unique to offer in the area of scholarship. They organized and duly began to advertise.

Hundreds of students sent in applications. Some wanted a degree in education. Others desired pre-law and premedical training; others opted for geology, meteorology, physics and the like. All applicants were refused entrance. The new university was not equipped to teach the subjects requested. You see, all twenty professors' doctorates were in minor tribal languages.

Some churches are like that. They know they have something unique and wonderful to offer the world. Yet they specialize in one area. Perhaps evangelism. Perhaps missions. Perhaps teaching. Perhaps social action. They are not well-rounded fellowships ministering the whole Truth to the whole person by means of a wide range of gifts in operation.

Alas, this is even more apparent in women's ministries. One could easily conclude that in Christ there *is* division between male and female[10] and the Holy Spirit has limited His gifts to women. In some places, the parameters of women's service are helping/serving, giving and teaching (restricted, of course, to other women and to those under 12 years of age!) If a woman's abilities and interest do not lie within these bounds, the church has no place for her special ministry. She is destined not to fulfill her mission in life or else to look beyond her church for outlets for her gifts.

Spiritual Gifts to Women

Since Scripture clearly calls women an heir of God and joint-heir with Jesus Christ[11] and a "fellow-heir of the grace of life"[12] with man, she is a first-class citizen of His Kingdom. That means she participates in the highest and best privileges offered by the King. These great benefits include the gamut of giftedness and ministry. The Bible gives witness to this, telling of female leaders, prophets, teachers, helpers and more.

What Are the Gifts?

What gifts may women expect to have? The Bible suggests several:

1. Prophecy
2. Serving
3. Teaching
4. Exhortation
5. Giving
6. Ruling/Leading
7. Mercy
8. Wisdom
9. Knowledge
10. Faith
11. Healings
12. Miracles
13. Discerning spirits
14. Tongues
15. Interpretation
16. Apostles
17. Administration
18. Evangelist
19. Pastor

Some biblical scholars include hospitality (1 Peter 4:9,10), celibacy (1 Corinthians 7:7) and martyrdom. Many believe the listings in Romans, 1 Corinthians and Ephesians are far from complete. Some even project a few of these gifts are not operable in the church today. It is not within the purpose of this book to deal at length with these issues. (See Resources for Deeper Study at the end of the book for more information.) Suffice it to say, the Holy Spirit is gifting all believers today regardless of race, age or sex; for "God is not one to show partiality."[13]

Defining Spiritual Gifts

A simple one-sentence definition of each of the gifts listed above is:

1. *Prophecy:* The Spirit-given ability to interpret God's revelation and proclaim it to others for the sake of action.

2. *Service:* The Spirit-given ability to give assistance or aid in any way that brings strength or encouragement to others.

3. *Teaching:* The Spirit-given ability to acquire and communicate truth so effectively that people are caused to learn.

4. *Exhortation:* The Spirit-given ability to come alongside another to help by means of a challenge, encouragement, or rebuke.

5. *Giving:* The Spirit-given ability to earn money, manage it well and wisely give for the Lord's work.

6. *Ruling/Leading:* The Spirit-given ability to influence, motivate and preside over others for the sake of achieving biblical goals.

7. *Mercy:* The Spirit-given ability to manifest practical, compassionate. cheerful love toward those whom the majority ignore.

8. *Wisdom:* The Spirit-given ability to apply biblical knowledge to life's situations.

9. *Knowledge:* The Spirit-given ability to search, systematize and summarize the teachings of the Word of God.

10. *Faith:* The Spirit-given ability to see something that God wants done and to sustain unwavering confidence that God will do it regardless of seemingly insurmountable obstacles.

11. *Healing:* The Spirit-given ability to intervene in a supernatural way as an instrument for the curing of illness and the restoration of health.

12. *Miracles:* The Spirit-given ability to perform acts of supernatural power, easily observable through the senses.

13. *Discernment:* The Spirit-given ability to distinguish between the Spirit of truth and the spirit of error.

14. *Tongues:* The Spirit-given ability to speak an unknown language or ecstatic utterance indistinguishable to both the speaker and the listener apart from interpretation.

15. *Interpretation:* The Spirit-given ability to interpret the utterance of tongues for the understanding and edification of others present.

16. *Apostleship:* The Spirit-given ability to minister transculturally with church-planting goals.

17. *Administration:* The Spirit-given ability to set present and future goals and to plan and implement the means to achieve goals for the advancement of Christ's work.

18. *Evangelism:* The Spirit-given ability to proclaim the Good News of salvation effectively so that people respond to the claims of Christ in conversion and in discipleship.

19. *Pastor:* The Spirit-given ability to guide, feed, and protect a group of Christ's followers.

If one includes *hospitality,* it is the Spirit-given ability to lovingly and cheerfully open one's home for those who need food, lodging and/or fellowship. Celibacy is the Spirit-given ability to be single and enjoy it. *Martyrdom* is the Spirit-given ability to suffer and even die for the Gospel, bringing glory to God through a victorious spirit.

Discerning Your Spiritual Gifts(s)

Once the gifts are defined, the next step is to discern which one(s) a person has.[14] What steps may one take to discover her gifts?

1. Begin with the spiritual gifts you would *like* to have. Don't confuse this with gifts you think you should have or that others expect you to have. Honestly, which gifts appeal to you? "The desires and aspirations you feel are caused by the very gift within you, pressing to be released in loving service," wrote James Davey.[15] By contrast, which gifts hold no appeal for you whatsoever? Why not?

2. List any *natural talents* and *abilities* you have. A woman who thoroughly enjoys teaching does not necessarily have a gift of teaching God's Word. However, it is not unusual to find natural skills complementing spiritual abilities. When you sing solos, do others repond in a way they do not respond to those whose voices perhaps have greater technical merit than yours? Perhaps your spiritual gift is being expressed through your music, a natural ability.

3. Think about that which *burdens* you. What part of church ministry concerns you most? Shut-ins? Newcomers to church? Battered wives? Unreached adults? Biblically-ignorant children? Disorganized meetings? Perhaps that which grabs your attention is a clue to your area of giftedness.

4. *Get busy.* In this case, you really learn by doing. Spectator saints don't discover their God-given abilities. They have to get into the game so to speak. In the playing they learn where they function best on the team. So experiment with a variety of ministries.

5. Listen to the *affirmations* of the spiritually mature. Has any Christian whom you respect as godly ever told you she believes you have a certain gift? Such feedback is worth hearing.

6. Determine the extent to which your various ministries are or were appreciated by others. "Learn by success or failure. . .When a pattern of giving others strength emerges, you have discovered a spiritual gift. Trial and error help eliminate the gifts you do not have."[16]

7. Determine your *enjoyment* and *satisfaction* in the performing of various services. Using your God-given abilities gives you a sense of joy and fulfillment. Peter Wagner calls this the "eureka feeling."

Develop and Use Your Gifts

Once you discover your spiritual gifts, look for opportunities to use them and ways to develop them. The latter may involve taking class work at a local Bible or secular college, attending seminars and/or asking to be discipled by one who has the same gift.

God does not take a gift back once He has given it. "The gifts and the calling of God are irrevocable."[17] *One may use, not use or abuse her gifts(s) but she retains the gifts(s). Yet how blessed the woman who develops her gift(s).*

To that woman Davey says, "You will discover the freedom there is in knowing how you may best minister to the Body.

There is release from fear of failure. You need not measure up to anyone else. You will revel in the liberty to do what God has equipped you to do, knowing that others are prepared to minister according to their gifts, making the whole complete. Learning your gift will take time. Using your gift will take the rest of your life."[18]

1. Complete the following statement for each gift you believe you have: "I know I have this spiritual gift because. . ."
2. For personal insight, how did you become a leader of women?
Primarily because:
____I am the wife of a church leader.
____I am a person willing to take the job.
____I had success in other "lesser" areas of ministry (a good Sunday school teacher "promoted" to superintendent).
____I'm just a girl who can't say no.
____I have gifts of leadership and administration which others readily confirm.
____It's what others seem to expect of me.
3. How did the workers in my church get their jobs? Review the four possibilities listed in this chapter.

Blessed is the woman who develops and uses her spiritual gift(s). Even more so, the church is blessed by the fulfillment of her God-directed ministry. But first we must be aware of our spiritual gift(s). If you haven't yet discovered God's special gift to you, the ability which He has designed for the building of His church through you, then stop here and search out this subject. If you never pick up this book again, it will not matter. The discovery, development and employment of your gift is needed by Christ's church, for its development and maturity. If you haven't already, take this exciting step today.

Many of you may have already discovered your spiritual gift, but haven't yet found creative ways to get it working. Pamela Heim's suggestions will be helpful to you, as will the following chapter: "Putting Your Gifts To Use," by Rick Yohn.

"Now that I know my spiritual gift, what do I do with it?"

"How can I exercise and train my God-given gift?"

Putting Your Gifts To Use

by Rick Yohn

One of the most exciting gifts I received as a child was a new bicycle. I was playing several blocks away from my house when suddenly a friend came running down the street shouting, "Ricky! Ricky! Guess what! I saw a truck pull up to your house and it had two new bikes in the back. And your dad helped the man unload them."

I yelled to my sister who was playing nearby and we ran home like jack rabbits. When we arrived, our mouths dropped open. Right before us stood two shiny new bikes. And they were ours.

At that point, the only obstacle facing me was learning to ride. I'd been on a bike only a few times, but within days, I was riding my new bike as if I'd been born on it.

This may be where you are right now. You've discovered what may be your gifts. You may be excited about your finding. And now you must learn how to use them effectively. Here are three fundamental principles to help you develop your discoveries.

Take Advantage of Opportunities

We could all be more effective teachers, singers, leaders, visitors, counselors, maintenance workers, and witnesses if we would take advantage of learning and training opportunities available.

Training Classes

Suppose you have the gift of leadership, but it is not at all developed. You want to learn how to lead and administrate. Perhaps your church holds leadership classes, or an evening school in your community offers administration courses. Sign up and see what happens.

If you have the gift of teaching or at least want to investigate the possibility, let this be known. Attend every teachers' meeting in your church, if they are available. Publishing houses often go into a community and offer one-day or weekend seminars. A leader or teacher who fails to attend training sessions hurts both himself and his ministry. There is always room for improvement.

If your gift is music, you will improve tremendously if you try to take private lessons and practice every day. If not that, you can still practice on your own or play or sing with groups. Choir rehearsals in many churches are more than practice for Sunday morning. They are times of training and improving voice quality. We should give God our best, rather than what is left over of our time and gifts. So look for some training program in your church or community and take advantage of it.

Reading

Do you realize that only 23 percent of the Christian public ever reads a book? Recently I talked with a friend from a Christian publishing company and asked him who reads their books. He replied that the progressive contemporary evangelical and the progressive contemporary liberal read most of the Christian literature. The hardened liberal (who denies everything and refuses to have anyone change his mind) along with the dogmatic fundamentalist (who has solved all the world's problems) do other things with their time. And then he added that about 80 percent of the readers are women. That's quite a commentary on the reading habits of the religious public. No wonder many Christians don't grow in their spiritual lives. If they don't supplement their Sunday diet with good reading material, their Christian vision remains embryonic.

Every gift that is found in the Scriptures can be developed through reading. You may say, "But I'm just a mechanic." Well, you can read magazines like *Popular Mechanics* to improve your gift. Read books on how to be a more effective teacher. Biographies of people like Helen Keller may challenge you to develop your gift of showing mercy. The biography of LeTourneau, Kresge, J.C. Penney, or John Wanamaker may stimulate you to use your gift of giving. Biographies of William Carey and other missionaries may ripen your gift of apostleship. A biography of George Müller will encourage your gift of faith.

You may not be able to attend a lot of training sessions or go back to school, but you can read. And if reading is agony because you're so slow, there are reading courses to help increase both speed and comprehension. It all depends on how serious you are with God. How committed are you to use your gifts?

Conferences

Conferences offer tremendous opportunity to develop gifts. A gifted teacher should attend Sunday school and V.B.S. workshops. When I was a Christian education director, I attended as many conferences as I could fit into my time and budget, because at these conferences I discovered new ideas and methods for teaching. You may want to improve your witness for Christ, or perhaps you want to know if you have the gift of evangelism. Try the various Lay Institutes for Evangelism throughout the U.S. and Canada. If you want to improve you leadership with youth, attend Bill Gothard's "Youth Conflicts" seminar.

School

Today many adults develop their gifts by going back to school. I'm not referring primarily to attending college as a full-time student, though in some cases this may be necessary. I'm thinking of night school or summer school, both of which offer an incredible number of possibilities.

Tapes

Another means of improving spiritual gifts is the use of tapes. With the cassette boom you can get information on just about anything. There are tapes to help you improve your musical ability, leadership, evangelistic ability, etc. Some tapes merely present factual material while others provide "how to " information. You can listen to tapes as you would listen to a transistor radio, while walking to school, while preparing meals, while you sun-bathe, or drive to the mountains. You may not have time to read a book, but you can probably find time to listen to a tape.

These are some of the resources available to you for developing your gifts. Some are more expensive than others. Some are more time-consuming than others. But don't excuse yourself from taking advantage of some resource.

Don't be satisfied with what you now know, or with past performance. Strive for excellence. Seek to improve. That's what growth and maturity mean.

Exercise Your Gift

It's evident that we can develop *knowledge* by reading, listening, and visualizing, but *gifts* and *skills* can be developed only by use. Ability grows as you put your gift to work. It's like a muscle. Neglect it and it becomes weak and flabby. Use it and it will perform usefully.

Recognize Value

This principle is especially helpful when your motivation is low. If you feel depressed or discouraged, you'll have little desire to develop your gifts. But if you realize the advantages of developed gifts, your motivation may increase.

Developed Gifts Provide Personal Identity

One of the major crises that most of us go through is the identity crisis. Who am I? Why am I here? Where am I going? This crisis has become a major problem in our depersonalized society.

God says that you are a gifted person with a divine mission on earth. You are necessary for the rest of the Body of Christ. And you will experience the truth of this as you discover your gifts and use them.

Developed Gifts Remove Unnecessary Guilt

Each of us experiences guilt to some degree at various times. The Sunday school teacher who fails to prepare his lesson, the father who refuses to discipline his children, the young person who yells at his parents, the Christian who bypassed an opportunity to witness: these are everyday examples of guilt. Sometimes our guilt is justifiable and other times it's unnecessary.

In *Guilt and Grace,* Paul Tournier describes two kinds of guilt: "true guilt," which is the result of disobeying God, and "false guilt," which results from the judgments and suggestions of men. We may make people feel guilty because of the way they dress or look or waste time or relate to others. We set up standards and expect others to comply. When they fail to achieve our standards, they sense our judgment and feel guilty. False guilt may also come from failure to reach our own goals, even if they are unrealistic.

Men have entered the ministry because their parents or some friend convinced them this was God's will. Eventually they drop out, and may feel guilt about their failure the rest of their lives. Some Christians accept church responsibilities because others felt they should, and if they are unsuccessful, they develop guilt. However, once you understand that God has gifted you, you have no reason for guilt. That is false guilt. It is unnecessary.

Developed Gifts Help You Become a Pace-setter

Many Christians merely echo what they hear. Too few really think for themselves. They have little self-identity. In contrast, the Christian who develops and uses his gift becomes a pace-setter. He isn't competing with other Christians. He isn't wasting his time comparing his results with the results of others. Instead, he is accomplishing what God has equipped him to do. In striving for excellence with his gift, he sets the pace for others. When he speaks people listen. He may even become an authority in his field.

Summary

As I conclude this chapter, I want to share a verse of Scripture that revolutionized my own attitude about God's working in my life. It has kept me from pushing ahead of God's time. It has removed the fear of "failing to make the grade." It has given me confidence that God has a place for me and will lead me in discovering it.

The passage is this: "A man's gift makes room for him, and brings him before great men" (Proverbs 18:16).

David's gift of music opened the door to Saul's palace. Philip's gifts of evangelism and miracles opened the door to Samaria. Paul's gifts of apostleship and teaching brought him to the Western world with the gospel. Elijah's gift of faith closed the heavens for three years, and brought him before King Ahab and the people of Israel. Bezalel's gift of craftsmanship built the tabernacle of God in the wilderness. Nathan's gift of prophecy brought him before David the king. Solomon's gift of wisdom brought great men and women of the world to his court. Peter's gift of exhortation caused 3,000 Jews to repent in a day.

God may not use your gift to bring you before great men. He may not use your gift in a way that the Christian world will sit back and admire. But be certain that he will open many doors for you to serve him.

"A man's gift makes room for him."

1. It's great to know that according to God's Word we each have at least one spiritual gift. How does recognition of this fact release me from the guilt feelings I sometimes have when I say, "No" to a task that someone in the church has asked us to perform?
2. What learning and training opportunities and materials are available so that I may learn how to use my gifts?
3. What opportunities exist in my church for me to develop and use my gifts? Where will my help compliment a ministry? What leader(s) can I talk to about becoming involved in ministry?

We acquire knowledge about our spiritual gifts by reading, listening and visualization. But knowledge about our gifts is like knowledge about God—it's of little use unless we do something with it. As we must personally know God, and not just have information about Him, so we must employ our gifts, and not just accumulate knowledge about them.

Our gifts, if they are to be developed, must become a part of our lives, and then not just on Sundays or other church assembly times. Our gifts can flow freely through us whether we are at home or at work, on vacation or in the hospital. What shines in the church should be no different than what shows in the home.

"How am I edifying the church through application of my spiritual gifts?"

"What are my motivations for involvement in my present ministry?"

Peace and Your Spiritual Gifts

by Rick Yohn

Chicago, Minneapolis, or Dallas would have taken it in stride. But an all-night thunder and lightning storm breaking loose in the sunny city of Fresno, California, made the natives extremely restless. No one slept well that night. Children scrambled frantically into their parents' beds. Lonely wives, isolated by a husband's business trip, clutched a pillow for protection. One teen-ager confided, "I thought it was the end of the world." And husbands consoling their wives nervously grinned, "It's just like a woman to get worked up over a little storm."

An unusual storm isn't the only cause of sleepless nights. For certain individuals, insomnia has become a way of life.

The Apostle Paul was no exception. He told the Corinthian church that he experienced "many sleepless nights" (2 Corinthians 11:27). Why? Probably among other things was "the daily pressure upon me of concern for all the churches" (11:28).

The Philippians had a personality problem (Philippians 4:2). The Galatians and Colossians were confronted with false teachers (Judaizers and Gnostics). The Thessalonians faced severe persecution. The Ephesians wrestled with the old self. The Romans abused their liberty in Christ. The Corinthians were plagued with all sorts of problems ranging from immorality to denial of the resurrection of the dead.

What about churches today? Peace becomes an impossible dream when certain individuals use their liberty to fulfill selfish desires. Peace disintegrates when one member threatens another or personality conflicts arise. Rather than seek peace, some pursue war. And one weapon of warfare may be a man's spiritual gift. With his spiritual gift he may destroy peace in his own life, his home life, and his church life.

This is why spiritual character is so important. Even though spiritual gifts don't guarantee peace, the character of God can govern use of our gifts in peace and for peaceful purposes. The fruit of the Spirit is peace. This peace must be integrated with our spiritual gifts.

Spiritual Gifts and Personal Peace

Moses had blown his chance at the Israeli *Who's Who* forty years earlier. Nobility, fame, power, and an unlimited future had vanished with his deadly blow to that Egyptian's head (Exodus 2:12). Now he'd spent the past forty years in the desert grazing sheep, when without warning a voice called out to him, "Moses, Moses! . . . I have surely seen the affliction of My people who are in Egypt . . . So I have come down to deliver them from the power of the Egyptians . . . Therefore, come now, and I will send you to Pharaoh, so that you may bring My people the sons of Israel, out of Egypt" (Exodus 3:4, 7, 8, 10).

God had gifted Moses with leadership ability, but the only leading Moses had done for years was confined to wandering sheep. Moses' first reaction to the offer, put in modern slang, was something like, "You've gotta be kidding! Why didn't you call me forty years earlier when I was somebody? People respected me then. They looked up to me. I had plenty of self-confidence. But now! There's no way I can go down to Egypt and lead a bunch of slaves out from under Pharaoh's nose." Moses had a gift, but he had no peace when he was challenged to use it for the Lord.

Most of us can identify with Moses. Though we're gifted in some ways we find it disturbing to use our gifts for the Lord. We may react with shock, "Who am *I*?" (Exodus 3:11). We may say we just don't know enough about the job to do it well (3:13). Then we think about all the things that may go wrong (4:1). We try to make it very clear why we aren't qualified (4:10). Finally, we admit that we'd honestly rather not do it because someone else could do it better (4:13).

Must we always go through this process when asked to serve the Lord? Is there no way in which you and I can experience personal peace when an opportunity arises to use our spiritual gift? Here are some principles to put into practice.

Be Certain That You Know The Lord

A God-given ability is no guarantee that an individual has experienced the new birth. A person may be a gifted musician without acknowledging his need of Jesus Christ. He may be eloquent in speech and yet blaspheme the name of the one who gave him the eloquence (Exodus 4:10, 11). If you've never accepted Jesus Christ as your personal Savior, peace will elude you. The Bible declares, "So now, since we have been made right in God's sight by faith in his promises, we can have real peace with him because of what Jesus Christ our Lord has done for us" (Romans 5:1, TLB). Without Christ in your life you remain separated from the one who gave you your gift, and you become burdened with guilt. Where guilt rules, peace cannot enter.

But here's good news. You can be freed from sin and guilt by accepting the payment Jesus made for you. He took your rap. You and I deserved death for our sins, but Jesus died in our place. God is satisfied with that payment for sin. The debt is cancelled. The Scriptures inform us that God "blotted out the charges proved against you, the list of his commandments which you had not obeyed. He took this list of sins and destroyed it by nailing it to Christ's cross" (Colossians 2:14, TLB).

If you would like to experience God's forgiveness, it is yours for the asking. The one condition is to confess to God that you have sinned against him and that you are accepting his Son's payment for your sin.

There is another problem to face, however. Peace with God does not mean that every believer is going to experience the peace of God when he is asked to use his gift. Even the Apostle Paul knew what it was like to confront a new challenge with fear and trembling (1 Corinthians 2:3).

Recognize That God Equips You For His Service

God will never ask you to accept a work for which he has not equipped you. It would be foolish for me to expect my ten-and-eleven-year-old sons to do the work of grown men. But I do expect them to clean their rooms, take out the garbage, and perform other household tasks suitable to their abilities (though not necessarily to their liking).

The military, the government, schools, and churches may bear the reputation of putting the wrong people in the right places, but God does not share that stupidity. The Bible makes it clear that we are not all suited for the same task. "Is everyone an apostle? Of course not. Is everyone a preacher? No. Are all teachers? Does everyone have the power to do miracles? Can everyone heal the sick? Of course not. Does God give all of us the ability to speak in languages we've never learned? Can just anyone understand and translate what those are saying who have that gift of foreign speech?" (I Corinthians 12:29, 30, TLB).

It is important for you to discover your gifts(s). For information on how to discover your gift(s) see chapter 11 of my earlier book, *Discover Your Spiritual Gift and Use It*. Once you begin to understand the equipment God has given you, make yourself available to opportunities where that gift can be used.

Moses claimed that he was not eloquent, but God told him that he was equipped to speak and then promised to speak through him (Exodus 4:10-12). If God has not equipped you musically, don't feel forced to sing in the choir in order to fill the ranks. If you have no concept of how to organize and motivate people to action, don't volunteer to be a leader just because there's a vacancy (unless it's a very temporary situation). Don't run away from any new challenge, but do consider the equipment God has given you and accept tasks suited to your gift(s).

Recognize That God Gives the Increase

Churches today are plagued with the "numbers racket." How many baptisms? How many new members? By how much did you raise the budget? How many new programs did you add to your Christian education outreach? Then as soon as we collect all the statistics we're supposed to send them to denominational headquarters and compare ourselves with the rest of the denomination. Or if we're an independent church we look around the city and pride ourselves for the number of sheep we've gleaned from the big denominations.

Obviously, a church has to grow if it's alive. I am challenged by church growth seminars. We should learn everything we can about the principles of sowing and reaping for the greatest harvest. But where we have to draw the line is in the area of unhealthy competition and comparison. It is ridiculous to compare the growth rate of a suburban church located in a beautiful, growing area with that of a country church surrounded by acres of cow pasture and near a town of 1,500 with ten other churches.

Over the years many pastors have developed an oversized inferiority complex, and the disease spreads into their churches. Small churches continue to think small and expect little, because they can't compete with their big relatives. The question is not "How big do we want to grow?" Nor is it "How big must we get to win the contest?" We must stop comparing ourselves to our denominational brothers and local neighbors and begin to measure our growth by the opportunities at hand.

Begin to ask, Why has God placed us in this location at this time? Who needs to be reached that no other church is reaching? Who needs to be counseled? Who needs encouragement? Who needs to be visited? Who needs the Savior? Who is being neglected by everyone else? Begin to answer those questions and claim these people for the Lord. Then you will experience both spiritual and numerical growth in your church. Further, design your methods around the needs of the people you're reaching.

If you're in a farm community, you may attempt some form of agricultural program in the church, a kind of Christian 4-H club. If you're in the inner city and ministering to minority groups, you might plan to develop certain skills. Look for those in the congregation who are gifted in craftsmanship. Or begin a bus ministry and employ those with the gift of helps as drivers. Perhaps your church is located near a university. The gift of teaching will probably be more available to your congregation than if you were elsewhere.

Methods differ. You may have more of one gift than another in your congregation because of the type of people who attend. You will also have a different rate of growth. This variety has already been mentioned in Scripture: "Now God gives us many kinds of special *abilities,* but it is the same Holy Spirit who is the source of them all. There are different kinds of *service* to God, but it is the same Lord we are serving. There are many *ways* in which God works in our lives, but it is the same God who does the work in and through all of us who are his" (1 Corinthians 12:4-6, TLB). But whatever ability, whatever service, and whatever method you use to reach people for

Christ, remember that blessing and growth come from God.

Paul rebuked the Corinthian believers for comparing one group of believers with another and explained how foolish it was. "Who am I, and who is Apollos, that we should be the cause of a quarrel? Why, we're just God's servants, each of us with certain special abilities, and with our help you believed. My work was to plant the seed in your hearts, and Apollos' work was to water it, but it was God, not we, who made the garden grow in your hearts. The person who does the planting or watering isn't very important, but God is important because he is the one who makes things grow. Apollos and I are working as a team, with the same aim, though each of us will be rewarded for his own hard work" (I Corinthians 3:5-8, TLB).

Thank God that he will never hold you responsible to do the work of another church or another person. He will reward you for doing what he has called you to do. He will bless you as you are faithful in performing the assignments he gives you. Whether that blessing is greater or smaller than another's is immaterial.

Keep the Needs of the People in Focus

Too often we confuse our objectives with God's purposes. God's purpose for giving us spiritual gifts is to meet the needs of others. We agree with this in theory, but in practice we may have other motives.

Why do our knees knock when we're asked to do something in public? Why does our stomach quiver and our throat tighten? Why do we break out in a cold sweat? Because we feel compassion for people and we're afraid we won't be able to help them? Let's admit that the number one issue at that moment is how we're going to appear in the eyes of others.

Preachers have this problem as well, but I've discovered how to minimize it. Whenever I begin to experience that nervous twitch, the queasy stomach, or the cold sweat, I focus on the needs of the people to whom I'm ministering. In fact, I have nerve enough to write a book only because I'm convinced that thousands of Christians need spiritual character to govern their spiritual gifts. If I weren't persuaded of the need, I'd find some other way to use my time.

Saturate Yourself With God's Word

The prophet Isaiah wrote many years ago, "Thou wilt keep him in perfect peace, whose mind is stayed on thee: because he trusteth in thee" (Isaiah 26:3, KJV). The psalmist confirmed that testimony: "Those who love Thy law have great peace, and nothing causes them to stumble" (Psalm 119:165).

This truth is especially significant to those who are gifted in preaching, teaching, evangelism, or exhortation. These gifts in particular are dependent upon firsthand knowledge of God's Word. A subtle temptation faces such individuals, however. The ministerial student studies the Bible from many perspectives. He takes Hebrew and Greek to understand the original languages. He spends hours learning Old Testament history. He studies the prophets, the Gospels, and the epistles, often with the purpose of passing future exams.

The temptation is to begin seeing the Bible as a textbook rather than the life-changing revelation of God, able to make the reader "wise unto salvation" and to equip him for God's service (2 Timothy 3:16, 17). It becomes a book of history, language, and facts to remember for the final.

A preacher may view the Scriptures as a supply house for sermons. A teacher may limit his study to, "This is what my class needs. I can't wait to tell them how to live!" An evangelist may never get past John 3:16 and the "milk of the Word" for his own life. The verses memorized and quoted by an exhorter to those he counsels may lose reality for himself.

On the other hand, a craftsman may think, "Why should I study the Bible? I'll never have to teach it. Besides, it's not that important in my line of work." A leader may begin to look to organization as the answer to all problems. One who shows mercy may feel that since he spends so much time in meeting the needs of the handicapped, God won't require any Bible study from him.

No individual is exempt from reading, meditating on, obeying, and sharing God's Word. The person who knows God's Word from firsthand encounter is far better prepared to meet the spiritual needs of others than one who is highly gifted but slack in his personal study.

God promises to bless his Word. "For as the rain and the snow come down from heaven, and do not return there without watering the earth, and making it bear and sprout, and furnishing seed to the sower and bread to the eater; so shall My word be which goes forth from My mouth; it shall not return to Me empty, without accomplishing what I desire, and without succeeding in the matter for which I sent it" (Isaiah 55:10, 11).

God promises to bless those who allow the Word to saturate their lives. "The whole Bible was given to us by inspiration from God and is useful to teach us what is true and to make us realize what is wrong in our lives; it straightens us out and helps us do what is right. It is God's way of making us well prepared at every point, fully equipped to do good to everyone" (2 Timothy 3:16, 17, TLB). Don't allow Satan to delude you into thinking that you can use your spiritual gifts and be filled with peace, while neglecting God's Word.

Pray Continuously

Most of us are success-oriented in one way or another. No one enjoys failing. Everybody wants to be a winner. But God would do us a disservice if he allowed us always to be successful in everything we attempted.

When we have repeated opportunities to serve the Lord, we begin to worry. "Will I be as good as the last time? Will people like what I do for them? I wonder if they'll accept me again. I hope nothing goes wrong. Will I have enough time? I don't think I'll be able to do it this time." Or if worry doesn't get to us, another temptation may. Ever depend upon past success for future success? It goes something like this. "Oh, this shouldn't be difficult. The last time I tried it the people really liked it. I guess I know the formula. Nothing to worry about. I'll just do exactly as I did the last time and everything should go great." The result?

Picking up the pieces of your shattered pride, you ask, "What'd I do wrong? Why didn't the people respond like the last time?" The answer is that the situation was not identical to the last time. The externals may have been similar. But think back on the last time. Remember how you committed the entire situation into the Lord's hands? Do you recall your attitude of dependence upon his Holy Spirit to work in the lives of the people? It wasn't the gift. Nor was it the personality. God declares, "Not by might, nor by power, but by my Spirit, says the Lord of Hosts—you will succeed because of my Spirit, though you are few and weak" (Zechariah 4:6, TLB).

If you want God's peace to prevail in your life the next time you're asked to get involved, then pray.

Acknowledge that your spiritual gift is from God (1 Corinthians 4:7). This helps remove pride from your heart.

Thank God that he has given you his character (Philippians 2:13). You will then be encouraged that some spiritual benefit can result.

Thank him for his control of circumstances. You can be assured that whether things go wrong (not according to your plan) or right (according to your plan), people will be blessed and God will be glorified.

Thank him that he has promised to meet the needs of people. This moves the responsibility from your limited capacity to his limitless resources and ability.

Ask God to receive the glory from your service, and really

mean it. Jesus said, "By this is my Father glorified, that you bear much fruit" (John 15:8a).

Finally, ask God to help you to relax in his Holy Spirit.

You'll be amazed with the results. Peace? Yes. Peace that goes beyond your imagination. No more depending on past success, the power of the flesh, the ingenuity of human wisdom, or the manipulation of people in order to succeed. Worries about being accepted and approved by others will begin to disappear. This type of praying will change you as well as others.

Paul described such prayer when he encouraged the Philippian believers, "Don't worry about anything; instead, pray about everything; tell God your needs and don't forget to thank him for his answers. *If you do this you will experience God's peace,* which is far more wonderful than the human mind can understand. His peace will keep your thoughts and your hearts quiet and at rest as you trust in Christ Jesus" (Philippians 4:6, 7, TLB).

What else could you ask for? Instead of your heart pounding as though it were about to break through your chest, it will be quiet and at rest. Instead of your thoughts dashing off into the realm of possible failure and embarrassment, they will be focused on the one who is going to meet the needs of people, receive the glory, and make you fruitful.

Practice What You Already Know of God's Will

Until God's will becomes a way of life with you, peace will be a hit or miss proposition. "Keep putting into practice all you learned from me and saw me doing, and the God of peace will be with you" (Philippians 4:9, TLB).

We may be using our spiritual gift for the Lord. But if we are griping or threatening or full of pride, we cannot expect God's peace to fill our lives.

God's will is expressed in hundreds of commands and exhortations throughout Scripture. As we accept these expressions of God's will and put them into practice when we use our gifts, God's peace will become a reality.

Spiritual Gifts and Peace in the Body of Christ

Spiritual gifts do not automatically bring peace to the local church. Some gifted teachers become extremely dogmatic. Like the Pharisees they "strain out a gnat and swallow a camel" (Matthew 23:24). Some who use tongues proclaim, "All must have it. Unless you have it you cannot be spiritual." Some even declare, "Unless you've spoken in tongues you can't be a Christian." Gifted musicians may fuss over how a certain number should be sung, or over who's going to get the leading part. Some gifted with exhortation may do a lot of rebuking without having all the facts. Any gift can be used in a way that produces disharmony and discontent instead of peace.

Biblical exhortations to maintain peace in the Body are abundant. "Let us pursue the things which make for peace and the building up of one another" (Romans 14:19). "And let the peace of Christ rule in your hearts, to which indeed you were called in one body; and be thankful" (Colossians 3:15). "Now flee from youthful lusts, and pursue righteousness, faith, love and peace, with those who call on the Lord from a pure heart" (2 Timothy 2:22). The following principles may help us achieve peace.

Keep in Mind Body Function

In some local churches Body function seems to be the responsibility of the "super saints." Statistics indicate that in many churches 20 percent of the people do 80 percent of the work. Imagine the problems you'd face if only 20 percent of your physical body were functioning. Is it any wonder that so many churches perform like invalids? It's because they are.

God never intended that the pastor do the work while the majority of the members sit on the sidelines cheering or booing. Body function includes 100 percent of the body members.

Paul wrote, "Under his (Christ's) direction the whole body is fitted together perfectly, and each part in its own special way helps the other parts, so that the whole body is healthy and growing and full of love" (Ephesians 4:16, TLB). Just as your mind tells your hand to scratch when you itch, and signals your legs and feet to cooperate so you can walk, Christ gives commands to the entire Body to function properly.

As Paul expressed it 2,000 years ago, "Suppose the whole body were an eye—then how would you hear? Or if your whole body were just one big ear, how could you smell anything? But that isn't the way God has made us. He has made many parts for our bodies and has put each part just where he wants it. What a strange thing a body would be if it had only one part! So he has made many parts, but still there is only one body. The eye can never say to the hand, 'I don't need you.' The head can't say to the feet, 'I don't need you'" (1 Corinthians 12:17-21, TLB).

As long as a certain group in the church does most of the work, there will be hard feelings, jealousy, self-pity, complaints, and criticisms. When the entire membership begins to use their gifts for the glory of God and the edification of the Body, peace is possible.

But what if there aren't enough jobs to go around? For instance, if you happen to be a member of a 2,000- or 5,000-member church, it's obvious that there won't be several thousand classes to teach. And the choir may be large enough already.

Perhaps the Lord will direct you to begin an entirely new ministry in the church: to the handicapped, or to specific professional or labor groups. It might include beginning a music school. Or you might want to train a group of boys or housewives in a basic mechanics program. If you take spiritual gifts seriously and are convinced that the church should help its individual members develop their gifts, you have a lot of room for creative programs. Too often we send our youth to ungodly musicians and then after a period of several years wonder why they're playing in dance bands and night clubs rather than in the church. We say that God has given the gift, we encourage our members to use their gift, but we ask the world to develop it. I am not advocating that we substitute a skills program for the preaching of the Word. Evangelism and edification must always be the basic objectives of the church. But edification isn't limited to the building up of spiritual life.

A second possibility when you face limited opportunities in your church is to use your gift outside the church building. The gifts are to be used for the entire Body of Christ as well as for reaching the world for Christ. You may be a professor who uses his gift of teaching in a faculty Bible study on campus. You may be a craftsman by gift and a designer or interior decorator by profession. Other churches in your city would greatly profit from your experience and gift. You may advise them or give them free labor in designing or decorating. When I lived in Winnipeg, a gifted craftsman, a contractor by profession, built our gym and educational unit and remodeled our sanctuary at tremendous savings to us. He wasn't a member of our church, but he was committed to using his gifts for the universal Body of Christ.

Your gifts might also be used in Christian schools, publishing houses, hospitals, companies, and in many other areas. Don't neglect your local church. But if the opportunities there are limited, don't neglect your gift.

A third possibility is to use your gift in another church. It's sad to see some large churches with highly gifted individuals warming pews, while smaller churches are crying for workers. Recently a church member came to me and said, "Pastor, you may have wondered where we've been the last two weeks. There's a small struggling church down the street from our house in the country. They really need help, and right now we're trying to decide what to do. We love our church. We've been involved in it for years. But since God has been blessing it so much and so many new people have come, we wonder if he might be able to use us better in the other church." I told him that I admired him for his insight and availability to God. Then I said, "Bill, you'll have to make the final decision. We'll miss you and your wife if you leave. But if you leave here to help a struggling work near your house, you'll go with our blessing and encouragement."

Function For the Edification of Others And the Glory of God

We have many reasons for getting involved in the Lord's work. Sometimes it's because no one else will do the job. At times we may feel that our involvement will help us gain favor with God. At other times it's to help us gain a sense of being needed. And sad to say, some just need to show others what they can do.

The Bible tells us that our primary objectives are (a) to build up the entire Body of Christ (1 Corinthians 14:4, 12, 26) and (b) to bring praise and glory to the one who gave us the gifts (Matthew 5:16).

A question I must continually ask myself as I minister with my gifts is, "Is anyone being helped by what I'm doing?" You've probably evaluated all you were doing at times and concluded that much of it was busywork. No one was helped or built up. No one praised God because of what you were doing. Nobody would miss the work if it were terminated.

If you discover that you no longer have time for your family, check for busywork. If your activity for the Lord is preventing you from spending time with him, consider it a warning signal. If you're beginning to snap at fellow workers and your patience is rapidly dwindling, it's likely that you aren't edifying the saints.

Once each individual begins to use his gift for the edification of the Body and the glory of God, peace will permeate the local Body. Alice won't argue with Barbara that she isn't getting enough solo parts. Instead she will sing to the glory of God and then thank the Lord that he wants to use Caroline next week for the same purpose. Don isn't going to be jealous because they asked Ed to build a pulpit for the front of the church. He knows that he will be able to make something else for God's glory at another time. Fred will thank God for the ten students entrusted to him to teach rather than jealously eyeing Gene's class of forty students.

God never gave us gifts to use for showing off ourselves to one another. If we commit ourselves to that truth, peace will prevail.

Encourage Peace in the Body

The Bible tells us to "pursue peace with all men" (Hebrews 12:14). Suppose you see a Christian abusing his gift. You can remain silent or you can confront him privately and deal with the problem.

We have a number of college students in our church. God has used them in a powerful way to encourage and challenge the adults in the congregation. The older members can sense the enthusiasm and freshness of these students. But once in a while an over-zealous one decides to straighten out the rest of the Body. When he pursues that task with fervor, peace in the Body is disrupted.

Often the motive of such young zealots is good, but their methods are wrong. Paul warned young Timothy about this problem. "Never speak sharply to an older man, but plead with him respectfully just as though he were your own father. Talk to the younger men as you would to much loved brothers. Treat the older women as mothers, and the girls as your sisters, thinking only pure thoughts about them" (1 Timothy 5:1, 2, TLB). God has called us not to "put down" but to "build up." If you see a gift being used improperly, deal with the issue privately and lovingly.

Another way to pursue peace is to become a "peacemaker." You notice that two members of your church are no longer talking to each other. Instead they have made it a point to talk about each other. You have the choice of sitting back and watching the sparks fly or you can ask God for wisdom as to how best to handle the problem. When such a problem arose in Philippi, Paul handled the situation himself. "And now I want to plead with those two dear women, Euodias and Syntyche. Please, please, with the Lord's help, quarrel no more—be friends again." Then he delegated the responsibility to a friend who was on the scene. "And I ask you, my true teammate, to help these women, for they worked side by side with me in telling the Good News to others; and they worked with Clement, too, and the rest of my fellow workers whose names are written in the Book of Life" (Philippians 4:2, 3, TLB).

The best approach may not be a personal confrontation by yourself. It may involve someone who is closer to the individual than you are. Whatever approach you use, remember that the purpose is to restore a broken relationship and not merely to rebuke the offense. Jesus said, "Blessed are the peacemakers" (Matthew 5:9).

We can have personal peace as we use our spiritual gift. We can experience peace within the Body of Christ as we use our gift. A third area where God wants us to experience peace with our gifts is in the home.

Spiritual Gifts and Peace in the Home

"Home, sweet home" is nothing more than a dream in many family circles. Dad runs down to church for the board meeting. The next night Mother is at her women's meeting. Another evening finds Johnny at his meeting and Jane's is the following night. Rather than complementing the ministry of the home, many churches are competing with it.

Besides programming something for everybody each night of the week, the church has a tendency to place church loyalty above family unity. The mother in the home may be a gifted teacher, but if she runs from one Bible study to another and neglects her family there will be little peace in the home. A well-meaning woman can create a serious barrier between herself and her husband by neglecting him.

How many gifted pastors lose their children? As they pass through the formative years and then the teen years, Dad is too busy to spend time with them. He is full of compassion, but it is poured out on others. He may be a gifted leader, teacher, evangelist, preacher, but his gifts produce bitterness and division in the home rather than love and peace.

Then there is the gifted craftsman or the individual with the gift of helping who spends all his time over at the neighbor's helping him. His wife pleads, "Sam, when are you going to stay home and get some work done around here for a change? Every time the phone rings and someone needs help you're out the door in a minute. But I've been asking you to do these chores for the past three months."

Use Your Spiritual Gift in Your Home

If the Lord has gifted you with teaching, consider your family as your primary classroom. Education began as a family matter. Moses told his people, "And you must think constantly about these commandments I am giving you today. You must teach them to your children and talk about them when you are at home or out for a walk; at bedtime and the first thing in the morning" (Deuteronomy 6:6, 7, TLB).

Perhaps God has given you the gift of craftsmanship. Does your home reflect that gift? A neighbor several houses up the street has a backyard second to none. When you walk into his yard, you get the feeling that you're up in the Sierras. Mountain plants and rocks garnish the yard. A stream flows from a nearby waterfall and drains into a beautiful pond sporting various breeds of fish. The air is filled with the chirping of birds. Under a large shade tree sits an old shed, equipped with a bed, old iron stove, a few chairs, and other antique paraphernalia. A landscape architect would have charged a fortune to duplicate the scene. But my neighbor used his gift of craftsmanship to accomplish this unique setting at a fraction of the cost.

Another gift that should be used in the home is the gift of leadership. What a waste for an individual who is skilled in organizing and planning to neglect his home. This gift could be used in establishing family budgets. It should definitely be used to manage a family with discipline and direction. One of the qualifications of a church leader is, "He must be one who manages his own household well, keeping his children under control with all dignity (but if a man does not know how to manage his own household, how will he take care of the church of God?)" (1 Timothy 3:4, 5).

Maintain God's Priorities in the Home

Man's first responsibility is not to be at the church preaching, teaching, helping, leading, exhorting, or singing. Nor is his primary role one of going into the world and preaching the gospel to the lost. God holds man responsible for being the head of his home. Paul writes, "But I want you to understand that Christ is the head of every man, and the man is the head of a woman, and God is the head of Christ" (1 Corinthians 11:3). Headship in the Scriptures is not synonymous with dictatorship. God is not saying that the man should be a tyrant over his household. He is saying rather that before the man decides to take care of his neighbors and friends and acquaintances he must care for his family. This means that next to his love for Jesus Christ, he must love his wife, not his church. The preacher who puts his church before his wife's needs may find himself taking his wife to the hospital because of a nervous breakdown. Or he may hear a judge declare, "Divorce granted." I don't mean to say that he should always pamper his wife. But he should be aware of her physical, emotional, intellectual, social, and spiritual needs and meet them as best he can (Ephesians 5:25).

Being the head of the home also means that the husband must provide for the family. "But if anyone does not provide for his own, and especially for those of his household, he has denied the faith, and is worse than an unbeliever" (1 Timothy 5:8). The context indicates that material provision is the primary emphasis. However, a child has the need to be loved, played with, and listened to. Merely providing food for the stomach and clothes for the body is not acting as a responsible head of the home.

The husband-father has a further responsibility as the head of the home. He is responsible to discipline his children (Hebrews 12:9, 10). Managing at the church is of secondary importance (1 Timothy 3:4, 5). Managing down at the office must also take a back seat to home responsibility. As long as the man in the family reverses God's priority system and puts church, job, or his own interests before those of his family, there will be little peace in the home.

Woman's first responsibility is to God. She is responsible to be a God-fearing woman (Proverbs 31:30; Matthew 6:33). Second, the married woman is to be a helper, suited to her husband. "And the Lord God said, 'It isn't good for man to be alone; I will make a companion for him, a helper suited to his needs'" (Genesis 2:18, TLB). Some women will say, "But my husband isn't a Christian. They need me down at the church." Or "The Bible study will fall apart if I'm not there." What are God's priorities for a married woman? She is to be a good wife. "Wives, fit in with your husbands' plans; for then if they refuse to listen when you talk to them about the Lord, they will be won by your respectful, pure behavior. Your godly lives will speak to them better than any words" (1 Peter 3:1, 2, TLB).

A third area of most women's responsibility is to be a mother. In many homes women reverse priorities two and three. Most of their time and interest are with the children. If there is any time, love, or interest left over at the end of the day, they may share some with their husband. Some women have gone this route by default. The husband is never home, so they might as well lavish their love and time on the kids. The big problem begins to show itself when the children leave home. A house that was once filled with a family is now occupied by two strangers. Notice the order given to Titus. "Older women likewise are to be reverent in their behavior . . . that they may encourage the young women *(a)* to love their husbands, *(b)* to love their children . . ." (Titus 2:3, 4). You are a wife first and a mother second.

But what about ministry to others? The Scriptures don't limit the woman to the home. She may have interests of her own (Proverbs 31:16, 20, 24). She may have a ministry to others such as teaching, counseling, visiting, exhorting, singing, etc., but—like the husband—she must not place these interests above the needs of her family. To redesign God's order of priorities is to tamper with your chances for peace in the home.

This truth applies just as much to children in the home. God does not place all responsibility upon the shoulders of parents. Children must share the burden. The Scriptures emphasize two priorities before self-interest. God must be first. Jesus said, "He who loves father or mother more than Me is not worthy of Me" (Matthew 10:37). If a parent were to tell his child to do something that was obviously contrary to the will of God, the child must make a choice. To obey his parent would be to disobey God. To obey God would mean disobeying his parent. Since the great commandment is first to love the Lord and then to love man (Matthew 22:36-39), the child would have to obey God.

But there is a second priority. "Children, obey your parents in the Lord, for this is right. Honor your father and mother (which is the first commandment with a promise)" (Ephesians 6:1, 2). As young children we obey our parents, but as we grow into adult life we honor them. The reason I dedicated my first book to my Dad was not to obey him. (He hadn't the slightest idea of my intentions.) The dedication was to honor him, to demonstrate in some tangible way how I've felt toward him over the years. Had my mother been living, the dedication would have included her.

A disobedient or dishonoring child brings no peace into a home. "Happy is the man with a level-headed son; sad the mother of a rebel." "A rebellious son is a grief to his father and a bitter blow to his mother" (Proverbs 10:1; 17:25, TLB). In recent years a group called the Children of God has tragically overemphasized the first priority to the complete neglect of the second. Young believers have been forced literally to forsake their parents. Brokenhearted parents have seen their sons and daughters walk out the door, never to return. No correspondence. No communication. This is not Christlikeness. Even at the end, as our Lord hung on the cross, he said to his mother, "Woman, behold, your son!" Then he said to the disciple, "Behold, your mother!" "And from that hour the disciple took her into his own household" (John 19:26, 27).

Spiritual gifts don't guarantee peace in our personal life. They won't automatically produce peace in the church or in the home. But they can be used in peace and for peaceful purposes. Being aware of these truths is the first step to experience God's peace. But the next giant step is to pay the price willingly, for peace will be realized only on God's terms, not ours.

1. *When I exercise my spiritual gifts, I rely upon (choose one):*
   past success
   manipulation
   prayer and God's power
   personal ingenuity
2. *How well has my church distributed its labors to different individuals? Does it operate on the "80/20" ratio?*
3. *Name an incident when you think that an individual whom you know abused his or her gift? Was the situation corrected? If so, was it handled in a peaceful and loving manner? If not, how would you have changed things?*

Our spiritual gifts, we must remember, are given by God for His glory and the building of His church. When I begin to take credit for God's graciousness, the entire body of Christ suffers. God has given spiritual gifts for the edification of the church. When they are used for that purpose they will bring glory to God and peace—not pride—to our hearts.

My ministry begins with the people closest to me: my immediate family, children, extended family and aging parents. The way I live my life may communicate as much to them about my Lord as the things I say about Him. There should be no contradiction between my lifestyle and my gospel.

"What does my lifestyle say to others about Christ?"

"How can I help my children to grow in an understanding of life and life's creator?"

Bequest of Wings
by Gladys Hunt

"I'm going to play in the Hundred Acre Wood," said the small boy who lived at our house.

I knew what he meant and where he was going, and so I said, "Fine. If you see Owl, be sure to ask him about Eeyore's tail."

We knew about Eeyore, Pooh, Piglet, Owl, and Christopher Robin. We had met them in a book[1] together, and our life would always be richer because they had become our friends. To this day I feel sorry for anyone who hasn't made their acquaintance.

That is what a book does. It introduces us to people and places we wouldn't ordinarily know. A good book is a magic gateway into a wider world of wonder, beauty, delight, and adventure. Books are experiences that make us grow, and add something to our inner stature.

Children and books go together in a special way. I can't imagine any pleasure greater than bringing to the uncluttered, supple mind of a child the delight of knowing God and the many rich things He has given us to enjoy. This is every parent's privilege, and books are his keenest tools. Children don't stumble onto good books by themselves; they must be introduced to the wonder of words put together in such a way that they spin out pure joy and magic.

I used to have an eloquent old journalism professor who would often exclaim rapturously, "Oh, the beauty and mystery of words! What richness can be conveyed by those who master them!" And while we jokingly recounted his dramatic incantations to our friends, we ourselves coveted the mastery of words, the symbols which convey ideas. We knew that what he said was true.

Take all the words available in the human vocabulary and read them from the dictionary, and you have only a list of words. But with the creativity and imagination God has given human beings, let these words flow together in the right order and they give wings to the spirit. Every child ought to know the pleasure of words so well chosen that they awaken sensibility, great emotions, and understanding of truth. This is the magic of words—a touch of the supernatural, communication which ministers to the spirit, a gift of God.

We cannot underestimate the use of words in creative thought! Proverbs says, "A word fitly spoken is like apples of gold in pictures of silver." The right word in the right place is a magnificent gift. Somehow a limited, poverty-stricken vocabulary works toward equally limited use of ideas and imagination. On the other hand, the provocative use of the right words, of a growing vocabulary gives us adequate material with which to clothe our thoughts and leads to a richer world of expression.

What fun it is to encourage a personal awareness of words in a child—the delight of sound, the color and variety of words available to our use. I am not suggesting vocabulary drills which teach by rote the meaning of large words. That is quite different than feeling the beauty of words. Books, the right kind of books, can give us the experience of words. They have power to evoke emotion, a sense of spiritual conviction, an inner expansion that fills a child to the brim so that "the years ahead will never run dry."

Books and experience go together. I delight in remembering the night we stayed late after a family picnic along an isolated lake in the north woods—far past normal bedtime for children. We watched the rosy glow of the sunset color the sky on the far side of the lake and darken the silhouettes of the trees. We felt the sand shed its warmth and take on a damp coolness. And then darkness came. We sat around the campfire and listened to the sounds of the night. Young ears picked up things older ears hadn't heard. What we heard we tried to express in words.

Deep-voiced bullfrogs far away, anxious peepers closer by, the gentle lap of the water on the shore, the loon crying in the distance, the crackle of the wood in the fire, the sparks going upward like brief fireflies. And then, as though it were a special gift from God, a whippoorwill, a shy bird usually heard only from a distance, lighted in the bush just behind us and startled us with his clarity of song. Later we watched the moon rise over the trees before going home. We felt beauty: we heard and saw it. We tried to couch the experience in words. Chatter does not enrich; the right words do. Well-chosen words need only be few in number, and they help store away the pleasure of the adventure.

We have often awakened a small boy at midnight to see the marvel of the northern lights. We have stood on hillsides and described the numerous shades of springtime greens across the landscape. It's a marvelous game of awareness and words.

It's a game that can be played anywhere at odd moments. *How do you think a barn in Nebraska looks?* One child may answer, "Red, with cows around it." Another may say, "Gray and lonely, with no trees near." A third child may light up and say, "The barn looks gray and tired, weathered from the summer's blast of heat and weary from icy winds that blow across the flat plains in winter."

Each answer is a good one. Yet those who saw less will be pleased by the contributions of those who saw more in their minds. They will sense the living substance of a touch of imagination and try to increase their own awareness. You may be thinking at this point, *I handle words so poorly myself. How can I help my children?* This game will teach you as well and bind you to your children as you share what we call "imaginings."

Try other questions: How does a summer night sound? How does a rainy day feel? What does a kindergarten child look like on her way home from school? I have done this in the classroom. Some children's contributions were dull and uninspired, some were hopeful, others had the bright shine of originality. But each child saw the "possibility of words." Natural gifts may differ and, like any other game, contributions should never be the only measure of a person's success. This is only one way of animating the mind in creative effort. But it will help train the ear to listen and the heart to feel beauty and emotion as it comes out in stories that the children later read. The benefits work both ways.

Reading aloud with two teen-age boys this summer, we discussed together the elements of writing which made the story so special. They went back through the chapter and found phrases that spelled out beauty like this, "I feel like spring after winter, and sun on the leaves, and like trumpets and harps and all the songs I have ever heard!" The words fairly ring with joy! I covet for both of these boys the ability to use language with the mastery of the author (J. R. R. Tolkien) whose book we were reading.

Since words are the way we communicate experiences, truth, and situations, who should know how to use them more creatively than Christians? The world is crying out for imaginative people who can spell out truth in words which communicate meaningfully to people in their human situation. And of all people on earth, committed Christians ought to be the most creative for they are indwelt by the Creator. Charles Morgan speaks of creative art as "that power to be for the moment a flash of communication between God and man." That concept opens up our horizons to a glimpse of God-huge thoughts, of beauty, of substance beyond our cloddish earthiness, of the immensity of all there is to discover.

Yet, tragically, Christians often seem most inhibited and poverty-stricken in human expression and creativity. Part of this predicament comes from a false concept of what is true and good. The fear of contamination has led people to believe that only what someone else has clearly labeled *Christian* is safe. Truth is falsely made as narrow as any given sub-culture, not as large as God's lavish gifts to men. Truth and excellence have a way of springing up all over the world, and our role as parents is to teach our children how to find and enjoy the riches of God and to reject what is mediocre and unworthy of Him.

Children are the freest and most imaginative of creatures. They love the fun of words and have a spectacular ability to learn. We must respect their eagerness and competence by introducing them to good books. I am frankly excited by the potential of books to build a whole, healthy, spiritually alert child who has the capacity to enjoy God and be useful to Him.

Emily Dickinson has winsomely captured the spirit of this:

> *He ate and drank the precious words,*
> *His spirit grew robust,*
> *He knew no more that he was poor,*
> *Or that his frame was dust.*
> *He danced along the dingy ways*
> *And this bequest of wings*
> *Was but a book. What liberty*
> *A loosened spirit brings!*[2]

Any good book can be used by God in a child's development, for a good book has genuine spiritual substance, not just intellectual enjoyment. Books help children know what to look for in life. It is like developing the taste buds of his mind as a child learns to savor what he sees, hears, and experiences and fits these into some kind of worthwhile framework.

What is unfamiliar becomes close and real in books. What is ridiculous helps children see the humor in their own lives. Sympathetic understanding is a generous byproduct of sharing the emotions of others in stories. Books are no substitute for life, but a keener pleasure comes to life because of books.

When you've walked across a field with an eight-year-old who comments on the "smell of sweet grass in a sunny pasture," then you'll understand what I mean. Or, "Dandelion stems are full of milk, clover heads are loaded with nectar, and the refrigerator is full of ice-cold drinks. Summer is very nice." Then you hear the words you read from *Charlotte's Web* come back to your own daily experience and agree, "Yes, summer is very nice."

This savoring of life is no small thing. The element of wonder is almost lost today with our mechanical devices and space-age living. To let a child lose it is to make him blind and deaf to most of life. Children have marvelous elasticity of mind. Fancy a child who hasn't met a dragon or a unicorn! Imagine a child who doesn't speculate about what small creatures might live in a hollow tree or rocky crevice! That's the stuff a sense of wonder may feed on, but when the child is older he will respond with the same sensitivity to a lovely sentence from Monica Shannon's *Dobry:* "Snow is the most beautiful silence in the world."

I have never been able to resist the appeal of a child who asks, "Read to me, please?" The warm security of a little person cuddled close, loving the pictures which help tell the story, listening to the rhythm of the words, laughing in all the right places as the policeman stops Boston traffic for the mother duck and her family in Robert McCloskey's *Make Way for Ducklings.* Or the safe, soothing feeling of Margaret Wise Brown's

Good Night Moon, or the wonder of Alvin Tresselt's *White Snow, Bright Snow.*

But the pleasure doesn't end with small children who like to sit on your lap. Growing-up children are just as much fun. Reading Laura Ingalls Wilder's books of pioneer adventure on the prairie, our family could feel the warm cabin, smell the freshly baked bread, hear the blizzard raging outside, and experience with Laura the close family feeling of Pa's singing and fiddling by the fireside. The love and gaiety of the Ingalls home were shared in our home, and we had a quiet confidence in a family's ability to surmount dangers and hardships.

Books *do* impart a sense of security. Children meet others whose backgrounds, religions, and cultural ways are unlike their own. They come to accept the feeling of being different, and fear, which is the result of not understanding, is removed. Geography invades our living rooms as children visit families from other countries, and the world seems quite friendly.

Facing failures and tragedies with the characters of a story may vicariously give children the experience of courage and loyalty. Weeping with some and rejoicing with others—this is the beginning of a compassionate heart.

Courage is transmitted by heroes like Johnny Tremain and even the comical Reepicheep in *The Voyage of the Dawn Treader.* Valor does not belong to an exclusive race of supermen. It is within the hearts of those who are committed to truth and honor, the kind of heroes with whom one can identify. Children have loved the biblical Daniel, David, and Joseph for these same reasons and have gained deeper understanding of the relationship of courage to faith.

One of my young friends read *Call It Courage* at least four times last year when he was nine. In transition between being a *child* and being a *boy,* he needed a model for his new manhood. This book fed his heart with ideals and integrity in such practical ways that it is difficult to measure its influence. He said, "It made me feel brave and strong!"

Every parent who reads with children and every teacher who shares books knows the wistful sigh that accompanies the request for "one more chapter." Because I love reading so much myself, I can never be too harsh when asked, "May I just finish this chapter?" even when I suspect that they are only on page two. I remember with special fondness the English teacher in my high school who sat on the corner of her desk and enchanted us with the music of Sir Walter Scott's *Lady of the Lake:*

> *The stag at eve had drunk its fill,*
> *Where danced the moon on Monan's rill,*
> *And deep his midnight lair had made*
> *In lone Glenartney's hazel shade. . . .*

Later, as a teacher myself, I knew the delight of taking children into a great adventure with a story—the utter silence of the room, the intent look on the children's faces, and the involuntary sign that escaped our lips at the conclusion of the episode. We had been together in the presence of good writing, and we felt bound together by the experience. My sojourn in that school was brief, but only recently a former student met me unexpectedly and eagerly told me what book she was reading. She could have paid me no greater compliment. Great literature has a way of building people. Books continue to be an influence far beyond my own words to these children.

What I am saying is simply this: As Christian parents we are concerned about building whole people—people who are alive emotionally, spiritually, intellectually. The instruction to *train up a child in the way he should go* encompasses so much more than teaching him the facts of the gospel. It is to train the child's character, to give him high ideals, and to encourage integrity. It is to provide largeness of thought, creative thinking, imaginative wondering—an adequate view of God and His world. He can never really appreciate the finest without personal redemption. But many a redeemed person lives in a small insecure world because he has never walked with God into the larger place which is His domain. We have books and the Book at our disposal to use wisely for God's glory.

A young child, a fresh uncluttered mind, a world before him—to what treasures will you lead him? With what will you furnish his spirit?

1. What are five books at my child's reading level that will excite him/her about imagination and language? Where can I find out?
2. What can I do to open the "tastebuds" of my child's mind? How can I make his/her world bigger?
3. What book-people have you introduced to your children (nieces/nephews, grandchildren) in the last few years? Think of three ways that you can do this during the coming year.
a.
b.
c.

God is involved in building a church that is whole, well-balanced and glorified in His own image. He calls this church His body. We, as members of that body, must ourselves be complete, vibrant and alive. As God nurtures His church, teaching it, correcting it, allowing it to fail and try again, loving it, so are we to train our children in the ways that God has ordained. The books we choose to read to our children form the way that they will see the world. The books that they themselves read will have an even greater effect, since they "discover" them for themselves.

From children we switch to single adults. Here too, lifestyle reflects our commitment to God. Are there people in the church who are excluded from fellowship with us because they are unmarried, divorced, widowed, or are married with children? Why do the differences in our marital status generally compel us to join groups of people with similar or identical status? How can we effectively step over those boundaries?

As we focus on single adults, let's keep other groups and individuals in mind. God overlooks no one. Neither should we.

A Growing Single Adult Ministry Responds to Good Biblical Content

By Britton Wood

A question often asked in single adult leadership conferences is, "How do you obtain names of singles not active in any church in order to enlarge your program?" This common concern majors on getting different persons involved rather than on caring for the persons already involved.

Value the Singles You Have as Members

The emphasis of caring for the singles already attending Bible study (Sunday School) is basic to growth. If the biblical content is meeting their needs, they tend to share with their friends that "I'm finding some help for my life here." Somehow the word gets around to different singles that "help is available at this place." Another way of expressing this feeling is, "Here is a 'good news' place."

If a singles ministry is committed to the concept that growth comes as people's needs are met, then patience will be part of the process. Growth is slow at the beginning, but occurs steadily. Also, the emphasis in all aspects of the ministry is to meet the needs of the persons who are active. It is important to go with the singles who choose to participate rather than attempting to build a program around the singles who do not desire to be a part of the ministry. The result of the latter situation is that some of the persons the leaders thought would respond do not; and persons the leaders had not thought about at all are the ones who respond. Rather than being disappointed in the persons who do not participate, the leaders need to be thankful for those who do participate.

After a meeting in our area, five or six singles approached me and shared the concerns of their group. They were concerned that their church didn't care for them and felt that they were leaderless. I suggested that they ask their church to allow the singles to do what they deemed important and to see what might happen. The singles responded by saying, "We already have the church's permission to do what we can." Then I suggested that they try to organize their group into some basic leadership areas and do what the group wanted to do in activities and Bible studies. They responded by saying, "Oh, we have officers; and we have good attendance at our activities and Bible study."

It seemed to me that this group was trying to minister to their real needs; they had over twenty persons involved. I commended them and encouraged them to relax, continuing to love and care for the people God had given them. In time he would give them some more people to care for and relate to, and they would be ready for them. Also, the church family would soon catch the spirit of the singles, and God's Spirit would open the doors that needed to open: whether those doors were marked more leadership, a larger facility, more church recognition, or a need in another area.

Care for the Singles' Personal Needs

It is possible to get singles to come to Sunday School without good biblical content, but it is difficult to get them to come back unless their needs are being met. Not only should the Bible study meet the single person's needs, but the people should care who he is. Basically the question is, Does this Bible study carry over into a caring relationship with *him?*

Some churches seem to have little problem in getting singles to initially become involved. Some of these same churches do not have a good stickability record. How many singles participate is not as important as what happens to the lives of these singles who do participate.

The mood of a singles group changes often, and the individual persons within a singles group change. Their needs also change; therefore, there should be a continual emphasis on evaluating the selection of Bible study curriculum.

Care for the Singles' Spiritual Needs

Although the quality of Bible study varies in our church, we try to always have helpful Bible studies. The quality of the Bible studies needs to be coupled with a caring membership (the singles) who show evidence of the love and forgiveness emphasized in the Bible studies. The numerical growth rises as the biblical themes are translated into caring action. In most of our single adult communities (departments), we have an ample number of singles to contact. So the way to get the names that most churches want is to meet the needs of the names (people) you have, and the people will come. Good content and genuine care are prerequisites for reaching out to persons not involved.

A question singles may ask is, "Where does all this Bible study take us, anyway?" Hopefully, Bible study helps us grow into the persons God wants us to become "in favor with God and man" (Luke 2:52).

Not all singles are alike in personality, reason for single status, or individual Bible study needs. It is imperative that a growing singles ministry learn that one particular diet of Bible study will not meet every person's needs. Single adults respond to Bible study best when the curriculum centers around their personal needs and focuses on how the Bible speaks to those needs.

Single adults have helped me understand that they have at least three basic needs as persons. Discovering what these needs are aids greatly in providing quality Bible study.

The Need for a Healthy Self-esteem

First, some singles have a low self-esteem or a low estimation of themselves. They don't like themselves because of the way they look, walk, talk, don't talk; because of their hair or lack of hair, their constant failures, their deep hurts that cause them to feel bad about themselves; or because of not fulfilling expectations at home or at work or with friends, of not having any friends, and many other reasons.

Persons in this category are generally so preoccupied with their problems that they don't have ears to hear. It becomes important to have Bible studies that *affirm* the person. Topics on love, acceptance, forgiveness, reconciliation, salvation, patience, and the weakness-strength tensions are most appropriate in assisting the person who has a poor self-image.

The Need for and Understanding of Self

Second, some singles have a healthy self-esteem. These persons are eager to better understand themselves. They are not interested so much in caring for others as they are in caring for who they are now and who they want to become. Areas of bible study that would appeal to this group are an emphasis on Christian liberation, Christian ethics, biographical studies of Old and New Testament personalities, the creation story, some of the psalms—any kind of biblical survey that helps the individual understand the Bible better and emphasizes self-identity, personhood, and the Christian growth process.

The Need for an Understanding of Others

Third, some singles have a healthy concern for others. These persons are anxious to know how to better relate to persons (both believers and nonbelievers), desire avenues of service within both the church and the community, feel a need to communicate better, and want to see other persons included in projects, activities, and helpful events. Some of the Bible studies that appeal to them include any emphasis on missions, personal witnessing, group interaction study, the Christian and politics, the Christian and moral responsibility, and studies concerning how Jesus related and responded to persons and situations.

Park Cities' Approach to Bible Study

In attempting to touch these various need levels in our Sunday-morning Bible studies, we have moved to offer electives or options (as an alternative approach to traditional Bible study curricula). Instead of having *a* teacher for *a* class, we have chosen a variety of themes. The teachers are selected on the basis of the theme, or the theme is chosen because the teacher was interested in that topic. The result is that leaders teach one particular topic (or study theme) for four to eight weeks. The Bible study is built around the needs of the group rather than around the personality of the teacher. We recognize that this is only one approach to Bible study, but the approach is working in our situation.

Another plus for this style of teaching is that persons who are exceptionally good Bible teachers are often available for a four-to eight-week period but, because of other commitments, would not be available for a full year's commitment.

One other benefit of this approach is that the singles become more flexible in their growth pattern and can learn from several teachers instead of just from a few favorites.

This type of curriculum format places the responsibility for the spirit of acceptance and caring on the group itself rather than on the teacher. So the group is committed to a growth process without having to wait on any particular teacher or leader. One of our singles who helps plan the curriculum for his community stated recently, "We just have Bible studies that meet our needs. We know what we need, and we just go after it. Our Bible studies have been terrific."

To meet all the spiritual needs of a growing singles group that is quite diverse is practically impossible. However, to recognize that all persons are at a slightly different place in their attitudes toward self, others, and God is a good place to begin to meet these various needs.

In our organizational approach (which, again, is only one approach), we have officers in each of our communities. The president and single adult council representative of each community (department) compose our single adult council. These persons are responsible (in counsel with the single adult minister) for choosing all the biblical content for our Sunday School.

Four Series of Bible-Study Sessions

We have chosen to have biblical studies each Sunday from each of four series or categories. *Series A* is *advanced* Bible study. This study attempts to follow a curriculum set forth with commentary notes from one of the Southern Baptist Sunday School Series. It can also include any in-depth study that enhances the Bible students' understanding of the Scriptures in a "dig-in" sort of study.

In *Series B*, we study any facet of *Bible survey*. The subject may be an overview of the Old and New Testaments, or it may be a survey of themes from the various sections of the Bible. This series is intended to help the new Christian understand the Bible better, as well as to help the Christian who has just become serious about being a learner.

Series C is wide open to any *Christian life concerns*. Helping the Christian live with a full awareness of what it means to be a Christian, relate as a Christian, cope as a Christian, share as a Christian, and care as a Christian are all parts of this important series.

In *Series D* the emphasis is on the *dialogical* (conversational). So often persons who want to relate their faith more clearly need to have a sounding board to help them express what they believe. This series is styled for small groups. In the small groups the opportunity to share and talk about the chosen topic is more readily available. This series generally enhances the *koinonia* (Christian fellowship) of the group and helps the participants to feel more accepted by God and the group.

An example of a particular Sunday Bible study offering for singles who attend Sunday School is:

Single Adult Bible Study

Our Bible study groups are formed by personal interest in selected topics or themes instead of being formed by age grouping. Please select the study you feel will be most beneficial to your life. Be sure to register in the room where your Bible study will be held, even if you preregistered for one of these studies. All studies will be continuing through this month. We prefer that you stay in one study, if at all possible, for the duration of the course.

SERIES A—Advanced Bible Study

What is Christian freedom? This is a study of the book of Galatians. The free theme in Galatians is not that of political freedom; it speaks of that freedom in Christ which is the spiritual basis for all true freedom. Among the key themes in Galatians are the gospel of grace, the basis for Christian fellowship, justification through faith, the meaning of Christian freedom, the fruit of the Holy Spirit, and the practice of Christian love.

Parenthood—Privilege and Responsibility. Parenthood is definitely an important responsibility. It is therefore important to have a healthy foundation in the way we approach our responsibility as parents. Single parents have a unique kind of responsibility. This Bible study is designed to be helpful to single parents and to potential parents.

SERIES B—Bible Survey

An Introduction to the Bible. This study examines what kind of book the Bible is, how it came together, what its unifying themes are, and what it says to persons today. Fuller understanding of the Bible as the Word of God can be a help to genuine faith.

SERIES C—Christian Life Concerns

Biblical Understanding of Self-Identity. Loving God and other human beings is contingent upon a proper regard for love for self. This study will focus on the understanding of self and the meaning of personhood, which the Christian faith expresses as valid and important.

The Christian Faith and Current Moral Dilemmas. This study will explore several current moral dilemmas and their implications upon Christian principles. Biblical insight and ethical teachings will be the emphasis of this study. Flexibility of the issues studied will depend on the participants and any new crisis that occurs during the process of this study.

Giving My Christian Faith Away—Naturally. This emphasis will give biblical insight regarding an authentic Christian witness. One's best witness occurs in the context of his daily walk. Certain understandings helpful to a genuine sharing of one's faith will be discussed.

SERIES D—Dialogue

Breaking Free. What does one's personal Christian liberty consist of? This dialogical study will explore, through selected biblical passages, the freedom to reminisce, relax, be content, share, ask, and go.

Some of the other Bible study ideas that have come from our curriculum study on the basis of need are:

What Did Jesus Say? This study will be an examination of some of the conversations Jesus had and what these conversations have to say to us about how we are to relate to Christ, how we relate to others, and how we relate to ourselves. This is a "dig-in" study. (Dictionaries, commentaries, and concordances are made available in this small-group research study.)

Hanging in There with Faith. Paul's charge to Timothy to keep the faith is a challenge to Christians of all times. It is imperative that we each understand what Paul's calling really means. This study will be concerned with Timothy and its relevance to today.

Faith in Action. "Faith without works is dead" is a familiar emphasis. We actually live our faith. What we choose to do or what we choose not to do depends on our faith. This Bible study will draw from the letter of James some "faithing" insights for our lives.

How to Be a Christian Without Being Religious. Are you religious? Do you sometimes feel you have been trapped into playing a game called "church"? This study speaks to religious hypocrisy; it shows why "religion" has failed and points to true Christianity and a faith that is valid for life. The studies are from Romans. (One resource is the book *How to Be a Christian Without Being Religious* by Fritz Ridenour.)

Old Testament Personalities: Their Faith and Their Lives. This Old Testament biographical study series will investigate the lives of Joseph, David, Solomon, and Esther. The intent of this study will be to better understand their faith and the motivation for living the kind of lives they lived, with applications to our lives today.

Sharing Christ in a Secular World. This study is a part of our Life and Work curriculum and will be dealing with such themes as "Marketplace Religion," "God's Expendables," "Why Go to Church?" and "Belonging to One Another."

Following Christ's Example—Interpersonal Relationships. This biblical study will center around the encounters Jesus had with both men and women, how he dealt with them, the results of these conversations in the lives of these people, and what we can learn from these situations about our own relationships with other persons today.

There Is Life After Birth—Now What? In this biblical study, effort will be made to examine the growth process of Christians from spiritual infancy to Christian maturity. The emphasis will basically be on how one can have a victorious Christian life in the midst of problems, conflicts, doubts, and disappointments.

What Do You Mean, I'm a New Creation? This biblical study will examine the beginnings of a new life in Christ and what it really means to become a new creation as a growing Christian.

Personal Friends of Jesus. This biblical study will center on persons whom Jesus knew and the concerns of their lives, including being faithful in the midst of life's perplexities, being a believer who doubts, being a believer who gets angry, being a believer who makes good decisions in life, and being a believer who knows the meaning of forgiveness. This study is part of our Life and Work Curriculum.

Three Stages of Salvation. A study of Romans 1-8. This a a concentrated study of the meaning of salvation and its freeing aspects. An excellent resource for Christians who want to dig deeper in the understanding of this most basic doctrine in the Christian faith.

How Can I Love My Neighbor Better—Or At All? This study will explore some of the reasons and possibilities for one's inability to "love your neighbor." Many times the "as you love yourself" portion of the Christian commandment (Luke 10:27) gives clues to our ability to "love our neighbor" better.

Prayer—Practicing the Presence of God. A biblical understanding of healthy praying. This series will explore the meaning of prayer, attitudes of praying, the question of answered and unanswered prayer, how we are to pray, developing a private prayer life, and resources for devotional readings. The leaders for this series are bringing their own understanding and discoveries regarding prayer as one Christian pilgrim to another. A different leader will be in charge each Sunday.

Determining Priorities for Life. A topical biblical study—how often is it in our lives that the "things we ought to do we don't do and the things we ought not to do we do"? This emphasis can give insight from varied life-style perspectives as to how some Christian individuals are personally working through choices and their own decision-making process.

Making It to Adulthood. This study will explore the shift in life that occurs from a dependence upon others to a joint responsibility with others. This Sunday the topic will be "Becoming the Adult Leader I Can Be." Recent high-school graduates are encouraged to attend this special emphasis.

The Living God and His People. This study is most appropriate for the beginning of the third century of our nation's life. We will study at least three major crises in the history of Old Testament Israel. Included in this series is "The Birth of a Nation" and "Covenant Faith Versus Pagan Culture." This study is part of the Life and Work Curriculum and can be most helpful for the person who desires to understand our Christian faith heritage better.

The Witness Within You. This will be an in-depth Bible study on God's Spirit within us. Much discussion in churches today deals with this topic. The approach of this study will be to examine closely what the Bible does say about how God works through us as Christians in areas such as: "Know the Holy Spirit," "Understand the Holy Spirit and Conversion," "Understand the Holy Spirit and Life's Greatest Venture," "Be Victorious Through the Spirit," "Allowing the Spirit to Be in Control," "Be Filled with the Holy Spirit," and "Continuing in Communion with the Spirit."

Moving Toward a Genuine Intimacy. This is more than a marital preparation study. One of the greatest needs that persons have in relationship with others is to develop an ability for closeness. The intent of this study is to explore openness and healthy closeness at this point of life—so that *if* marriage occurs, we will not be distant persons in the midst of such a relationship.

In-depth Bible Study. This is a free-lance Bible study with some definite direction. This in-depth material is for singles who want to "dig in" on some pertinent biblical topics. "Study to shew thyself approved unto God, a workman that needeth not to be ashamed, rightly dividing the word of truth" (2 Tim. 2:15).

Do You REALLY Know Christ? A study of 1 John, with an emphasis on three tests that help us *know* we are followers of Christ. The tests are moral, social, and spiritual.

Studies in James: Lessons in Daily Living. This study will explore problems of trials in life, the demand of a true religion, responsibilities of teachers of the faith, problems in interpersonal relationships, problems of presumption, problems of affluence, the coming of the Lord, the importance of work, and the power of the church at prayer.

Applying the Gospel. Most Christians need a more complete understanding of how to apply the gospel in a way consistent with daily living. This study will include three emphases: (1) "Applying the Gospel: Its Relevance," (2) "Applying the Gospel: Its Biblical Base," and (3) "Applying the Gospel: Its Social Implications."

Facing the Future with Hope. This topic is the last portion of a study of the living God and his people in the Life and Work Series. The emphasis of these Old Testament studies will be on "What if the Worst Comes?," "Coping with Change," "Keeping the Faith," and "Sustained by Hope."

What the Bible has to Say About Marriage, Divorce, and Remarriage. This study explores the meaning behind these sayings: (1) "They lived happily ever after," (2) "Divorce is the unpardonable sin," and (3) "A divorced person who remarries commits adultery." The subject then turns to what the Bible says about these three topics.

The Christian Single and the Current Political Scene. How can we, with good insight, face these election days with more than a political bias? This Bible study will examine the Christian's responsibility to authority, the attitudes of leaders, and some actions Christians might take. This study will have different leaders each Sunday, each of whom is capable in this field.

When Christians Pray. This Bible study is designed to challenge single adults to give more attention to prayer responsibilities through consideration of the meaning, nature, and purpose of prayer.

The Christian's Responsibility Regarding Money. Money management is part of our stewardship of life, and this Bible study is intended to give added insight to one item—money—which causes many of us much anxiety. Our attitude regarding money can make quite a difference in our daily decision making.

Telling Others About Christ. Witnessing is more than preaching and teaching, and it is a vital theme for today's Christians. The Bible and the needs of society make witnessing a priority task; yet, for one reason or another, many professing Christians make no serious effort to witness for Christ. This study will give a better understanding of biblical teachings about the role of Christians and churches in today's world. (A Life and Work study.)

Living and Sharing in Christian Joy as God's People. As God's people, we place great value in studying the Bible effectively and evaluating our prayer life in the light of New Testament models. This Bible study series is intended to help us share more completely in the joy of Christ's coming and to encourage joy in daily living. This study is part of the Life and Work Series.

Jesus and His People. This study will correlate the Old Testament prophecy as it relates to Christ's earthly mission, the effect Jesus had upon the people (his disciples) around him, the effect Christ's Spirit had on other New Testament people, and the effect of Jesus on us today.

Digging In with Some Scripture Heavies. This study will give opportunity for the participants to share in some familiar but profound Scripture passages. The selections for this four-week study are specifically geared to self-examination as to "how I'm cutting it in my Christian life." There will be some participant research tied in with this study. The four topics are: (1) "How Is Your Love Life?' (2) "Back to Basics," (3) "How Is Your Equipment?" (4) "Making the Tough Decisions." (A Serendipity series.)

God's Intent for Us—Christian Living and Giving. This study will involve God's original intention for his created order and man as the climax of this creation. This emphasis will also deal with how sin marred God's original purpose for creation and for man. The climax of the study will help us learn how God in his divine redemption seeks to restore the created order and man to his original purpose for them.

Meeting the Need for Personal Growth Through Bible Study

A good indication that the Bible study is meeting needs is the request for more intensive studies. More singles are wanting to gain biblical insight, and some are embarrassed that they have been coming to church most of their lives and are now learning things about the Bible and the Christian faith that they never knew or heard before, One person commented, "I could have stayed there [his class] another hour."

One of the helps I seek to give our singles has to do with diet. Encouragement is made to vary our Bible teachers so that more nourishment is given to a greater number of persons. The examples of some of the bible study themes are indications of variety. Much more variety is now possible because of the genuine hunger of the single adults.

A tension that accompanies the singles' opening themselves to God's Spirit and beginning to feed on God's message to them in the Bible is a feeling of dissatisfaction. A dissatisfaction with self is a part of this attitude. For the first time in many singles' lives, God is very personal; and they are getting a taste of the joy of following Christ. The question "Why didn't someone help me see this before?" rises. It is possible that several persons (pastors, parents, teachers, friends) had attempted to help this person see certain aspects of the Christian faith; but only now is the person willing—in fact, eager—to learn (to be a disciple).

Another dissatisfaction a person may feel is that many persons around him are not as serious about the Christian life and studying the Bible as he is. It is interesting to see a person become hungry; he sometimes thinks all other persons *should* be equally anxious to learn. Most persons are prone to feel that what is happening to them *ought* to happen to everyone else *now,* and in almost the same way. Patience is, once again, the Christian fruit that needs developing here. If other persons who were growing spiritually before this individual got "turned on" had been as critical of him as he is of others, he might never have had his eyes and ears opened to God's Spirit.

The Christian Single: a Learner and a Minister

The more one learns about Christ and the Christian pilgrimage, the more he sees that there is to learn. Part of being a disciple is to be a learner. There is always a need for more spiritual understanding and growth. In a sense, the stance of the Christian needs to be that of one who is somewhat frustrated about what is yet to be learned. Full satisfaction that allows one to rest on what has already been learned misses the mark of the Christian.

Good biblical content and a caring spirit will come with the growing desire of the single adults to minister verbally or to take action in mission service. Bible study that does not bear fruit in a relational way misses its intent. Consider trying to fill a sponge with water and not squeezing the water out of it before using it. Sponges are helpful when an emptying effect takes place first. Christians are vessels that need to spill over into the lives of others.

The style of teaching the Bible to singles is important. Some singles want an authority to tell them how to live their lives. Others do not want anyone telling them how to live. What is of prime importance here is for the teacher not to yield to either position, but to yield to the Holy Spirit as authority.

Importance of Space Facilities

The facilities available to a singles group can make a difference in the approach taken in the Bible study period. Generally, singles prefer to be in a large coeducational grouping rather than in small classes. This arrangement provides some anonymity for some who are uncomfortable reading the Bible aloud or praying aloud in a group. If the department or class is not too large, the members will feel more at ease in sharing personal concerns related to the Bible studies.

If a facility could be ordered for a singles group and placed at Park Cities Baptist Church, I would want a large, open, carpeted room that would have round tables for discussions or informal fellowship time and also have adequate space for large-group settings. It would have a piano and numerous bulletin boards and chalkboards; the walls would reflect a cheerful attitude. There would be a magazine resource section, containing a few soft chairs that would provide an adequate setting for semiprivate counseling, committee meetings, or casual reading. It would also be helpful to have a sink deep enough for washing and filling a coffeepot and a refrigerator for some food and soft drinks or juice.

One important consideration regarding any new singles group in a church is to keep the group located in the main educational area if at all possible rather than placing them in a house or similar facility away from the main area. Many churches relegate a singles group to "the little house" across the street and go right on with the ministry they were doing before the singles needed a place. When the singles are placed in the mainstream of the life of the church, they become a part of the whole church earlier; and this arrangement also eliminates the attitude of some singles that "the church has put us over here out of the way."

When a singles ministry has a healthy identity among its members, moving to a house or new facility especially designed for the singles would not be harmful.

The facilities and the location of the facilities that a congregation provides the singles ministry say much about the church's attitude and vision. Churches need to carefully plan with the singles in mind rather than protecting the favorite spots in the church for the nonsingles.

The facility does not make the biblical content great, but it does affect the attitude of the persons who come for the Bible study. The care given to a facility that singles use can be but one expression from the whole congregation that says, "You have worth; we care for you."

1. Who are the singles in my church? Name three you'd like to know better.
a.
b.
c.
2. Your church non-verbally communicates "we care for you" or "we aren't interested in you" to its single adults. Choose one of these assumptions and share with another person ways that your church does/does not care. How could it be improved?

3. What can I do to affirm singles in my church? Who, specifically? What other groups (senior adults, widows, teens, etc.) or individuals might I (we) be overlooking?
4. Identify one way your group has translated Biblical themes into caring action?

Society imposes distinctions in marital status upon us in a way that distorts God's perspective. Remember Paul's words to the churches in Galatia?: "There is neither Jew nor Greek, slave nor free, male nor female, for you are all one in Christ Jesus" (Gal. 3:28). Marital distinctions do exist, and they do affect the way in which we relate to other people, but the Lord would have us to be impartial in our Christian fellowship, worship and discipleship. Singles, senior adults, children and our church friends are all connected and related to us in the body of Christ.

With singles, as with all others, our lives should be transparent. People who see us should be able to recognize the God-in-us, as well as the mother, teacher, executive, mechanic or whatever. A transparent life will often appear to others as a "simple" life; one in which the priorities are in their proper order. Our lifestyle can have a strong influence in how we meet our third priority—reaching out to the needy people of this world.

"Is my present lifestyle the way it is by habit, gradual development or conscious choice?" "What words would I use to characterize a "simple lifestyle?"

Evangelism And Simpler Lifestyle

by Gladys Hunt

"This new reality [entering the Kingdom of God] places men [and women] in a position of crisis—they cannot continue to live as if nothing had happened; the Kingdom of God demands a new mentality, a reorientation of all their values, repentance.... The change imposed involves a new lifestyle."[1]

The gospel demands change. New life, new lifestyle. Evangelism is not the preaching of a new lifestyle. It is the preaching of new life; it is the good news about Jesus. Lifestyle is another matter. Logically and ethically it is the *fruit* of the good news naturally and purposefully enhancing the evangel. We want to examine here the relationship between lifestyle and the preaching of the good news.

What is a Simple Lifestyle?

I must confess to great confusion of mind and heart when I ask, What is a simple lifestyle? Simple compared to what? H. L. Hunt, the Texas multimillionaire, carried sandwiches to lunch in a brown bag every day—sandwiches made of bread made from wheat from his fields, ground and baked in his kitchen. The seats in the leather chairs in his office sagged and the living room in his home overlooking the lake in downtown

Dallas wore a dingy 1930 beige. Did he live a simple lifestyle? Or was frugality merely part of his eccentricity? And what cause prompted his penurious ways?

Another person receives acclaim for driving an ordinary Ford (and that one four years old) while others in his income bracket drive Cadillacs and Lincolns. Certainly that is simpler and less ostentatious.

Another shops at five different supermarkets to get the best prices. Or haunts the thrift shop periodically to get good used clothing. Or scours the bins behind supermarkets to salvage food that has been tossed out. Is that what we mean by a simple lifestyle?

Or what of the mother who tears apart an old shirt, laboriously clipping all the stitches, pressing out the seams, fitting the patterns to make a new skirt for her smaller daughter. Time-consuming, yes. But wasteful, no. Is that what it means to have a simple lifestyle? And what do such things have to do with evangelism?

I could go on. Simplicity takes many shapes and forms. No fertilizer for the lawn. Moving to the country and growing your own vegetables and cutting wood for your fires. Biking instead of driving. Baking instead of buying. Freebies for entertainment.

Two problems distort discussions about simple lifestyle: a tendency to legalism which leads to pride, and an inadequate theology about possessions. Legalism wants a monolithic style. During the late 60's I invited a campus rebel to our home for further conversations (which were later incorporated in a book on contemporary student opinions called *Listen to Me*). When he arrived in our ticky-tacky subdivision and rang the bell, almost his first words were "I'm surprised to find you living here." He had his idea of where someone who thought the way I did should live: a flat near campus like his—with plants in the windows instead of curtains, pillows on the floor and one shadeless lamp in the corner, complete with onion smells wafting up the stairwell. How could I possibly live where I live with all the needs in the world? It was simply not appropriate to live in a subdivision. He seemed not to consider his high rent, magnificent stereo, record collection, ten-speed bike and the cost of justright jeans. Concern for the world, it seems, must have a certain look, a certain style.

Simple lifestyle in those terms becomes faddish, almost cultic. And of course some of the protestors of the late 60's and early 70's have joined the establishment and are now accumulating the "good life."

Simple lifestyle is not a way to cop out of social relationships and responsibilities. Many of the specifics that mark simplicity might also mark selfishness or a stingy spirit. Phyllis McGinley in her book *Sixpence in Her Shoe* explains it delightfully:

> Thrift is neither selfishness nor cheese-paring, but a large, compassionate attribute, a just regard for God's material gifts. It has nothing in common with meanness and is different even from economy, which, although it may assist thrift, is a habit rather than a moral act. . . . Economy saves pennies, trims corners, and has a tidy mind. . . . The poor receive economy's handouts, but they will be relentlessly entered on a tax return. Meanness ruthlessly stints the table, lets others pay the check, and when it gives old coats to refugee committees, cuts off buttons and fur collars. Thrift is something else again. When thrift serves stew to the family to ease the budget, it sees to it that the dish is savory as filet mignon and it delights to share with anyone who comes to the door. It is never stingy and antlike. Thrifty is a preserver rather than a hoarder and rejoices in hospitality.[2]

We should be sure, then, that our discussion of simplicity in lifestyle first means a lifestyle-for-others—simple so that it can truly honor others and meet their needs. As one woman said, "Life is too short to stuff a mushroom."

Second, our theology gets tangled in emotions. We feel guilty because we wonder if we are possessed by our possessions.

We suspect that is true, but we lack the courage to investigate reality. Our view of God is bound to affect us. Is he an austere, parsimonious Being who wants to take away all that is beautiful and comfortable, a kind of bare-room monastic God? After all, the Son of man had no place to lay his head. He never married. He borrowed a donkey when he needed it. He fished for money. Others supplied his needs, but he did have a robe good enough for soldiers to gamble for it at the foot of the cross. So what conclusions do you want to draw?

Some people assert that the Scriptures say very clearly that God has given us all things richly to enjoy. Human prosperity is the blessing of God. He who gave elaborate instructions for the building of the temple with its intricate work of gold and silver, its carvings. He is the one who has placed in us a love of the beautiful, and has sanctioned our personal collection of some of the good things of this world. It is true that God is extravagant with both beauty and joy. He is almost wasteful with seedpods, butterflies and sunsets. Imagine a God who gives ten verses in the book of Job to the glory of the hippopotamus and thirty-four verses to the crocodile. Imagine a God who gifts a Bach and a Beethoven to conceive such magnificent sounds. He makes artists and poets. "Glory be to God for dappled things," Gerard Manley Hopkins wrote.

But God is also willing to lay down glory. He humbled himself, took on human form and became obedient—even to death on a cross. He gave his life for ours, that we might know his righteousness.

So what does glory and humility have to do with lifestyle? I prefer to talk about *obedient lifestyle* rather than simple lifestyle. We are not committed to simplicity. We are committed to the Lord of the universe. Can those who claim to know him not care about what is on his heart?

To be unconcerned that our rising affluence is crippling already poverty-stricken nations should be unthinkable. One-third of the world's population consumes three-fourths of the world's protein every year, and we are part of that one-third. A different third of the world's people has an annual per capita income of $100 or less. We cannot ignore the cry of hungry neighbors.

But we dare not be unconcerned about spiritual famine either. Our spiritual lifestyle is often as extravagant as our material lifestyle. A kind of spiritual greed for experiences, a euphoria about truth, has thousands going from conference to convention and across town to another meeting. Many Christians live in a cozy subculture enjoying group-think.

We are often as oblivious to empty hearts around us as we are to empty stomachs. All around us—in our neighborhoods, our cities, across our country and around the world—are people with hollow hearts. They have simply never heard the evangel.

The purpose of this paper is to examine the relationship between a simple lifestyle and evangelism. How can a simple lifestyle enhance, encourage, aid, hasten, affect evangelism?

A Simple Definition of Evangelism

John R. W. Stott gives a simple definition of evangelism: "Evangelism is sharing the good news with others. The good news is Jesus. And the good news about Jesus which we announce is that he died for our sins and was raised from death and that in consequence he reigns as Lord and Savior at God's right hand, and has the authority both to command repentance and faith, and to bestow forgiveness of sins and the gift of the Spirit on all those who repent, believe and are baptized."[3]

I believe that biblical evangelism is adequately defined by Stott's statement, although I'm aware that some would include additional elements in such a definition. That is not to say that evangelism meets all of a person's needs in God's sight. As Bishop John Taylor has said, "A hungry man has no ears." Hungry people need physical bread. Scripture is clear: "If anyone has material possessions and sees his brother in need but has no pity on him, how can the love of God be in him?" (1 Jn. 3:17 NIV). Biblical evangelism is not in opposition to meeting social needs. As Ron Sider says in his monograph *Evangelism, Salvation and Social Justice*, evangelism and social action are equal and full partners in the mission of God's people. Both are necessary. Neither is an excuse for the other. Each stands in its own right. Each demands *presence* to some degree, but action, servanthood and communication must accompany meaningful presence in either.

Evangelism is simple obedience. Jesus told us to *go, tell, teach*. Social action is simple obedience too. Together they are a full-orbed expression of discipleship. People are not bodiless souls or soulless bodies. We must try to be as holistic as our earthbound vision allows us to be.

The Lausanne Covenant states that "in the church's mission of sacrificial service evangelism is primary." Our purpose here is not to argue the validity of that statement but to underscore that human beings without Christ are without hope in this world and the next, that alienation from God has eternal consequences. That fact needs to grip us until we hurt a little, not so that we frenetically assume God's responsibility but that we willingly obey the Commander.

Practical Issues

The Commander has the program. He is ultimately the enabler. Has he, in fact, enabled us to do something about the evangelization of the world?

First, and most obviously, we can personally obey his command to evangelize. Generally we want to respond in every way but that: give, send, pray. If every believer "gossiped" the gospel out of a convinced heart at every opportunity, the evanglization of the world would be well on its way. Until simple obedience is our first concern, our primary need is for repentance.

Second, we can fund a great army of those who will preach the good news. Why is the church of Jesus Christ allowing young people to itinerate the length and breadth of the land with a tin cup, as it were, pleading for support to allow them the privilege of going to share the message? They have been trained; they are ready to go. What delays their going? They have not raised their support. Why isn't the church out looking for those who will go, ready with funds, already having prayed that the Lord would send forth laborers?

Instead we find travel-weary candidates, beholden to hundreds of supporters, spending too much time cultivating contacts to bring in dollars that will allow them to obey God's call. That happens regularly in independent mission boards and increasingly with denominational boards. It is called the personal touch, justified because it works and because of the prayer support supposedly engendered by the contacts. But it also encourages a personality cult. The man or woman fit for tribal work may have a quiet, persevering way, not given to public speaking or easy social expression. It may take such a person twice as long to raise support.

Pragmatically, raising one's own support "works," which keeps people from asking if it is according to truth. It encourages the church to feel benevolent when the church has, in fact, been penurious. It fosters a double standard: one standard of living for believers who go and another standard of living for believers who stay at home. What would happen if the members of the body voluntarily assumed a minimum standard of living (not legislated, but decided before God individually) and gave the rest of their income to the mission of the church in the world? The first thing that would happen would be the revelation of our idols—do we serve God or mammon? And that would bless us all.

Fuzzy thinking about commitment has to be dealt with if the church is to obey the command to go and tell. Os Guinness in his book *In Two Minds* speaks of people who move smoothly through three levels of understanding and still leave out something essential. It is possible for persons to know their need, to know that Christianity provides an answer and that Christianity is true, and still believe inadequately because they have never fully committed themselves to Christ.[4] Our Lord Jesus knew that our view of earthly possessions most clearly defines our commitment. It did with the rich young ruler. He went away sorrowful for he had many possessions.

The means to reach the world might be in hand if believers simply tithed. "The gulf between what affluent Northern Christians give and what they could give is a terrifying tragedy. *Christianity Today* reported recently that a *mere tithe* from the fifty-two largest U.S. denominations would be $17.5 billion annually. Instead they gave only $4.4 billion in *total church giving* in 1971."[5] "Total church giving" is not necessarily money to help either the poor or the unevangelized. Suppose the church gave $17.5 billion; that would still be only a tithe. We need to break through with fresh urgency. Even the Old Testament economy of the law had tithes and *offerings;* surely the economy of grace urges us to explore more than tithes. "Freely you have received, freely give" (Mt. 10:8 NIV). God holds us as accountable for what we keep for ourselves as for what we give. Jesus still stands by the treasury.

The amount of money that would be available for a needy world if all believers scaled down their standard of living excites the imagination. Glory would be given to the name of God not only from the expansion of his kingdom but from the purifying of it. What hinders believers from the carefree lifestyle Jesus was talking about in the Sermon on the Mount ("Take no thought. . .")? Is it that we derive our sense of wellbeing from what we possess? Do our possessions reassure us of our worth? Surely that is sub-Christian thinking. Is it anxiety about the future? It is true that God is not honored by a failure to plan, but he is less honored by unbelief. How much it must please God when those who say they know him then trust him with their lives and possessions.

Third, we can rethink our strategy and let go of our money. The church and individuals often give gifts that are not truly gifts. We want to control what we give. We have strings attached. Some feedback, some strokes are necessary to make us feel good about giving. Our money can be used for *this* but not for *that*. I am not suggesting careless or thoughtless giving. Hard-nosed evaluation of strategy and quality of work marks godly giving. We need prayerful planning, not simply impulse giving (yet pity the person who never feels the impulse of the Spirit to do something spontaneous.) What I am saying is that if the world is to be evangelized we have to expand our vision of who will do it and how it will be done and let go our money to do it. We need to ask how the job can best be done.

Waves of change continually affect the missionary enterprise. Americans today cannot go to some places; we are not the best choices to send to others. But we are often woefully provincial in our concern for the world. We pray appropriately for our missionaries, our denominational outreach, or whatever. And there it ends. We need to pray for the whole church—for the planting of the church, the growth of the church, the health of the church. Who prays for the places where we can't send anyone? Who will use the news of the world as a prayer reminder? We must rid ourselves of a colonial attitude, of any trace of benefactor—and we must be willing to use our resources wherever the need is.

For instance, I am impressed with the project undertaken by the Langham Trust fund, where key African and Asian nationals receive support in theological training in England to further the work of the church in their country. Or the Jubilee Fund which provides support for national mission development in various places in the world, keeping believers in their area and sharing the gospel.

The new evangelical seminary in Central Africa Empire may well provide a key to evangelizing Francophone Africa. That seminary is the vision of an African leader, Byang Kato. Who supports such a broad venture in an area where the church is weak and barely supports its own pastors? Or what of the evangelical seminary outside Paris, which meets an urgent need for first-rate education for French pastors?

Assam has closed to missionaries. Nationals have taken over all the facets of work once done by Baptist General Conference missionaries. The church is young and needs teaching to face the persecution it now is experiencing. The BGC is supporting Assamese broadcasts and Assamese personnel to broadcast from Sri Lanka. *Africa Enterprise* supports African evangelists, helps needy refugees in the name of Christ, supplies money so that Ugandan Christian students who are studying abroad can complete their education and be ready to return home when the present trial is past. The list could go on.

The creative possibilities are far greater than anything we know about. We need to release funds to internationally supervised programs or to projects devised by nationals which meet legitimate needs and which could further the work of evangelism in an indigenous way.

Someone will warn about the danger of "rice" Christians, those who might respond to the gospel because of the offer of food or shelter. Not at all! We need to trust the national church, not cripple it. I believe we have not been nearly creative enough in working closely with national leaders to equip their own people in the work of evangelism.

Beyond that we need a fresh call to incarnate the gospel wherever the Lord calls us personally. We have allowed our need of possessions and the finery of life to separate us from the neighbors in our own communities. We salve our conscience by giving to a missionary offering instead of sharing the gospel with a neighbor. Visions of lands far off; blindness for those at home. The love of things can keep us from going across the street or to any other hard place to obey Christ. Yet he remains the supreme example—the laying aside of what was rightfully his and humbling himself to become obedient.

Our possessions make us increasingly immobile. The idea of incarnating the gospel in primitive circumstances is hard. The problems of health, sanitation and safety in the slums of the world's cities threaten those who go to live among them. It may be that some will die, which society will call tragic wastefulness. Mother Teresa took the risk of not developing immunities, as did Granny Brand in India. Our confidence in a God who counts such "waste" as fragrant worship needs to increase. We need to ask that great biblical question, Is anything too hard for God?

Does living in the inner city or the wrong neighborhood for the sake of Jesus strain God's ability to take care of his own? Our possessions may be pilfered by the people we are trying to reach. The more we have, the greater the risk. Our best efforts may be spurned, our person mistreated. Is that too much for God or us? Many more need to stay in changing neighborhoods or to live in the hard places at home for Jesus' sake.

Think how many American Christians live in spacious homes with perfect decor—sterile places where few outsiders are ever welcome. Unused rooms, unused clothes in the closets, a freezer full of food, tennis rackets, bikes, soft drinks by the carton—and a tight social schedule that doesn't allow time for people who live in other spacious homes on the same street. Lost people include those who are poor and those who are rich and those who are in middle-class America. Our hospitals, nursing homes, retirement centers, jails, juvenile homes and shelters for runaways and battered wives—all are full of desperately hurting people. Some people don't need to move; they need to open their eyes, unclutter their lives, empty their closets and open their homes for Jesus' sake and share his goodness and love. The need to communicate the gospel is not limited to any geographical location. Only our vision is limited.

In many places the witness of the gospel needs to be strengthened by the demonstration of a community, a community that lives and preaches the good news about Jesus. I believe specialized ministries like that are carried on effectively in large cities across the world, and their number could increase. The words of one support the testimony of another. Openness of lifestyle invites others into the center of the community to show a drastically different way to think about life.

My point is this. Our obsession with the material world can paralyze our best intents. It takes time and energy to maintain and enjoy too many possessions. Concern for a needy world, a world that dies for lack of knowledge of Christ, becomes the least of our concerns. Dom Helder Camara in *Revolution through Peace* says, "I know how very hard it is to be rich and still keep the milk of human kindness. Money has a dangerous way of putting scales on one's eyes, a dangerous way of freezing people's hands, eyes, lips and hearts."[6]

I know this too, and I mourn my earthiness, my frozen hands, eyes, lips and heart. We all need to hear again our Lord Jesus say, "I am the light of the world. He who follows me will not walk in darkness, but will have the light of life.... If the Son makes you free, you will be free indeed" (Jn. 8:12, 36). And then we need to realize that we have been made *light* in a needy world and pray that we will have the freedom to use our possessions in spreading of light, instead of being used up by them.

1. Think of someone who has learned to live creatively in a simpler life-style. How do you identify this person? What do you think are his/her priorities?

2. Is my present lifestyle the way it is by habit, gradual development or choice? What is God telling me about my present lifestyle?

3. To me, what specifically characterizes a "simple" lifestyle?

4. What "mushrooms" in my life are unnecessary to stuff?

Afterword

If you could describe the Christian woman of the next decade, what would she be like? To attempt to answer this question might be an exercise in futility, except that the woman who is a child of God has some exciting qualities that no one else can claim. As an individual, she is a person whom God has created in His own image, with the same uniqueness that He bestowed upon each flower, each snowflake, each drop of rain. He has endowed her with beautiful qualities which, though sometimes undeveloped, have the potential of transforming her own life and the lives of those around her. God's creative act makes her a person with the courage to believe in herself, the freedom to fail and the sensitivity to reach out to others in ministry.

Within her, God has designed the capacity for a growing relationship with His Son, Jesus Christ. Her strength, desires and self concept all flow freely outward from this relationship. She knows that she is important to God, to her family, to other people in her life and to herself. She is sprung free from her "sameness;" she confidently uses the gifts that God has invested in her person, because He is her creator, encourager and guide. She is aware that He has placed her on His earth for

His purpose, and in His love she both recognizes and responds to her vocation as a servant.

The Christian woman is a person that "wears more than one hat." She is not limited to the four walls of her home, although her ministry at home is a high priority. She is knowledgeable, well educated through the experiential phases of life as well as through the formal training she may have received. She is not willing to let sorrows and inequities pass by without the healing touch of her hand. She arises to meet needs and enlists the aid of others who know and serve her Lord. She is not afraid of changes that may affect her lifestyle. She is ready to act when the moral and spiritual health of her community are threatened.

And there is more. She is a role model who is aware of her impact on the lives of those around her. With her husband, she teaches and nurtures her family in the basic concepts of the Christian faith. She enriches her life through the many avenues of study, both individually and in group settings. Her priority for such enrichment comes from her study of God's Word. She is aware that she is an example for other women, new believers and those who do not know Jesus Christ.

The Christian woman keeps her priorities in their proper order: commitment to God, relationship to her family and the Body of Christ, ministry to people. She is creative in a way that makes her life enjoyable, pleasing and attractive to others. Her lifestyle is characterized by obedience to God and His Word. She discovers her place in the ministry of the church as she discovers and exercises the gifts that God has given to her. She is a true servant of God, who models the characteristics found in the Beatitudes. She is a person who is free to be herself because she is created in the likeness of God.

After reading this book you may well determine that it is impossible to be the "wonder woman" that seems to be described. Yes, it is impossible, and no one person could attain all the qualities that you have discovered in these chapters. But that is where the challenge begins. With God's help you can step out of your sameness, your life of routine, your ministry that seems dull, your growth that seems to stand still. You can accept the challenge by praying, "Lord, I can be the kind of woman that you want me to be. But I can't do it by myself. You are my Lord and only you can change me. I am willing to be changed. I am afraid, I am not sure of myself, I don't know what changes are in store for my life. But you, Lord, are bigger than me—you know my heart. Take me, mold me and make me to be your obedient servant, your changed woman."

What a challenge! Will you accept it? Will you allow God to continue His rebuilding of your inner spirit? Will you accept the ministry that He may have for you? If so, then you are already becoming the "impossible woman" that we've described! With thousands of others you can say, *"Yes, God . . . I Am a Creative Woman."*

My prayers are with you as you seek to know His will.

Dorothy Dahlman

Resources For Deeper Study

These resources will enable you to further explore the concepts that you've discovered in *'Yes, God...I Am a Creative Woman'*.

Who Am I? (chapters 1-4)

Hunt, Gladys. *Ms. Means Myself.* Grand Rapids: Zondervan Publishing House, 1972. "Every woman has the potential for more basic personal freedom and fulfillment than she now experiences." The author not only lives the principles taught in her book, but has enabled others to achieve these goals through her teachings and writing.

Landorf, Joyce. *Changepoints.* Old Tappan, NJ: Fleming H. Revell Company, 1981. A spiritual road map to guide you through the turning points in your life—no matter what extremes of turmoil they present. Transition times such as getting married, becoming a mother, losing your job, a crippling accident, are times that require adjustment. What will God do with these changepoints in your life?

Malcolm, Kari Torjesen. *Women at the Crossroads.* Downers Grove, IL: InterVarsity Press, 1982. A path beyond feminism and traditionalism. Traces women's contributions to the church from Christ's time to the present and applies her conclusions to single and married women today.

Neff, Miriam. *Discover Your Worth.* Wheaton, IL: Victor Books, 1979. Lack of self-esteem keeps many women from achieving Christian womanhood. This biblical perspective considers our unique personhood, our relationships with others, and our source of power, freedom and direction.

Ortlund, Anne. *Disciplines of the Beautiful Woman.* Waco, TX: Word Books, Publisher, 1977. It takes work to become the disciplined woman that you want to be, but life is exciting when we know we're living up to God's expectations.

Stott, John R. W. *Christian Counter-Culture: The Message of the Sermon on the Mount.* Downers Grove, IL: InterVarsity Press, 1978. This careful exposition of the Sermon on the Mount accurately expounds the biblical text and relates it to life today. The author says he wants to let Christ speak this sermon again, this time to the modern world.

Swindoll, Charles R. *Improving Your Serve: The Art of Unselfish Living.* Waco, TX: Word Books, Publisher, 1981. The subtitle says it well. Accurate, clear and practical help from the Scriptures on how to develop a servant's heart. The author says you don't have to be brilliant or gifted to pull off the truths in this book; but you do have to be willing.

Foundations (chapters 5-7)

Briscoe, Jill. *Prime Rib and Apple.* Grand Rapids: Zondervan Publishing House, 1976. A series of thought-provoking interactions between Omnipotence (God) and various women of the Old and New Testament. Each chapter brings out a unique characteristic of God, highlights the potential of the individual and implies action for the reader. Excellent discussion material.

Foster, Richard J. *Celebration of Discipline: The Path to Spiritual Growth.* San Francisco: Harper & Row, Publishers, 1978. An interesting book concerned with the inner life; giving attention to what the author calls the inward disciplines, outward disciplines and corporate disciplines. Based on the Scriptures and draws from classics of devotion and secular thinkers.

Getz, Gene A. *Building Up One Another: How Every Member of the Church Can Help Strengthen Other Christians.* Wheaton, IL: Victor Books, 1977. More than just philosophy. An expression from the pastor of a growing church, who emphasizes both Bible and "body life." The author discusses 12 significant "one another" commands of the New Testament, with practical helps which allow every member to take part in building up other Christians.

Little, Paul E. *Paul Little's Why & What Book.* Wheaton, IL: Victor Books, 1980. Two of the author's volumes *(Know Why You Believe* and *Know What You Believe)* have been combined in this volume. This book has led people to Christ, sharpened the knowledge of their faith and helped new believers understand their faith. It will answer the questions that challenge your belief, and in a way that will strengthen your Christian life.

Packer, J. I. *Knowing God.* Downers Grove, IL: InterVarsity Press, 1973. Answers questions as: What were we made for? What aim should we set for ourselves in life? What is the eternal life that Jesus gives? What is the best thing in life? What in man gives God most pleasure? The author says that ignorance of God—both of His ways and of the practice of communing with Him—lies at the root of much of the church's weakness today. A book for serious study and discussion.

Pippert, Rebecca Manley. *Out of the Saltshaker and Into the World.* Downers Grove, IL: InterVarsity Press, 1979. More than a personal testimony. A series of helps to enable you to relax, to be open and honest about your life in Christ.

Yohn, Rick. *Getting Control of Your Inner Self. (See next page).*

Ministry and Skill Development (chapters 8-10)

Christenson, Evelyn. *Gaining Through Losing.* Wheaton, IL: Victor Books, 1980. How everyday hurts and crushing tragedies can be turned into unbelievable spiritual gains. Her seminars draw people from all walks of life and help turn their attention toward the God who created them and can make them spiritually richer. She speaks from the Word of God, with applications from personal experience.

Heim, Pamela. *The Ministering Woman.* Arlington Heights, IL: Harvest Publications, 1980. The author touches Christian women who want to be part of some ministry, but need encouragement; she gives biblical principles to follow and guidelines for personal and group study. For women who want to be involved in ministry, who want to understand the biblical foundations for their ministry, and who want to involve other people.

Landorf, Joyce. *Mourning Song.* Old Tappan, NJ: Fleming H. Revell Company, 1974. The author's mother told her, "Honey, for thirty-four years I've taught you how a Christian should live. Now, I'm going to show you how one dies!" The author stirs the soul toward the realities of not only the dying of others, but of one's own death, as well.

Mains, Karen Burton. *Open Heart—Open Home.* Elgin, IL: David C. Cook Publishing Company, 1971. How to find joy through sharing your home with others. This material is basic to understanding Christ-centered hospitality, whether you are male or female, young or old, married or single. It has the potential to change the way you live.

Yohn, Rick. *Discover Your Spiritual Gift and Use It.* Wheaton, IL: Tyndale House Publishers, 1974. Dr. Yohn examines the gifts mentioned in the New Testament in the context of biblical meaning and contemporary applications. A warm, informal, practical handbook to help you minister for Jesus Christ.

Yohn, Rick. *Getting Control of Your Inner Self.* Wheaton, IL: Tyndale House Publishers, 1982. Now published by Rick Yohn. This volume explores the realm of Christian character and shows clearly that what we are is even more important than what we do. He implies that it is the maturing Christian character that governs the use of our spiritual gifts.

Lifestyle (chapters 11-13)

Aldrich, Joseph C. *Life-Style Evangelism*. Portland: Multnomah Press, 1981. A study of personal and church life-style evangelism. The author uses Jesus Christ as the Christian's personal model, and the church model found in Acts 2. For personal enrichment and use as a group study in women's ministries, especially for the leadership team.

Dayton, Edward R. and Ted W. Engstrom. *Strategy for Living*. Glendale, CA: G/L Regal Books, 1976. How to make the best use of your time and abilities. You can use what you have learned from life to decide what it is that God wants you to be and to do. Set goals, establish priorities, do your planning and start living. The result can be a whole new approach to living!

Foster, Richard J. *Freedom of Simplicity*. San Francisco: Harper & Row, Publishers, 1980. "Models of simplicity are desperately needed today. Our task is urgent and relevant. Our century thirsts for authenticity of simplicity, the spirit of prayer and the life of obedience." These are comments from an author who points the way for Christians to make their lives "models of simplicity." Good for personal study and group discussion.

Hunt, Gladys. *Honey For a Child's Heart*. Grand Rapids: Zondervan Publishing House, 1978. The imaginative use of books in family life. For parents who are concerned about whole children—who are alive emotionally, spiritually and intellectually. She shares great treasures she has found in books and The Book.

Sider, Ronald J., editor. *Living More Simply*. Downers Grove, IL: InterVarsity Press, 1980. Biblical principles and practical models. Chapters on topics ranging from Old and New Testament foundations for simple living, to contemporary economics, professional ethics and evangelism. A book that will encourage living more simply.

Wood, Britton. *Single Adults Want to Be the Church, Too.* Nashville: Broadman Press, 1977. Understanding single adults and working with them to meet their needs through the church. From a pastor who has majored in this ministry. Who singles are, what their needs are, how to work with them, with models provided at every stage of planning and action.

Notes

Chapter One
1. See Raymond C. Ortlund, *Lord, Make My Life a Miracle!* (Glendale, CA: Regal Books, 1975).
2. Vernard Eller, *The Simple Life* (Grand Rapids, MI: Eerdmans Pub. Co., 1973), p. 21
3. ©Copyright 1976 Anne Ortlund. All rights reserved.
4. ©Copyright 1972 Anne Ortlund. Used by permission.
5. See Anne Ortlund, *Up With Worship* (Glendale, CA: Regal Books, 1975).

Chapter Two
1. Jerry White, *Honesty, Morality & Conscience* (Colorado Springs, CO: NavPress, 1979), pp. 81, 82.
2. William Barclay, *The Gospel of Matthew* (Edinburgh: The Saint Andrew Press, 1956), 1:86.
3. Augustus M. Toplady, "Rock of Ages, Cleft for Me," (1776).
4. "Man a Nothing," taken from *The Valley of Vision: A Collection of Puritan Prayers and Devotions,* Arthur Bennett, ed., (London: The Banner of Truth Trust, 1975), p. 91.
5. Bernard of Clairvaux, "Jesus, Thou Joy of Living Hearts," trans. by Ray Palmer.
6. Dag Hammarskjold, *Markings* (New York: Alfred A. Knopf, 1978), p. 53.
7. Archibald Thomas Robertson, *Word Pictures in the New Testament,* vol. 1 (Nashville: Broadman Press, 1930), p. 41.

Chapter Three
1. William Barclay, *The Gospel of Matthew* 1:98.
2. Leslie Flynn, *Great Church Fights* (Wheaton, IL: Victor Books a division of SP Publications, Inc. 1976), p. 44.

Chapter Four
1. Clyde S. Kilby, *The Aesthetic Poverty of Evangelicalism.*
2. *Honey for a Child's Heart* (Zondervan, 1969).

Chapter Eight
1. 1 Corinthians 12:1, 7 *(NASB)*.
2. Galatians 3:28 *(NASB)*.
3. Nancy Hardesty, "Gifts," *The Other Side* (July-August 1977), p. 40.
4. 1 Corinthians 12:11 *(NASB)*.
5. Matthew 16:18.
6. Leslie B. Lynn, *19 Gifts of the Spirit* (Wheaton, Illinois: Victor Books, 1974), p. 13.
7. *Ibid.*, p. 200.
8. Peter Wagner, *Your Spiritual Gifts Can Help Your Church Grow* (Glendale, California: Regal Books, 1979), p. 37.
9. Elizabeth O'Connor, *Eighth Day of Creation: Gifts and Creativity* (Waco, Texas: Word Books, 1971), p. 15.
10. Galatians 3:28.
11. Romans 8:17.
12. 1 Peter 3:7
13. Act 10:34 *(NASB)*.
14. For an excellent individual or group study in greater detail, *Spiritual Gifts and Church Growth,* Fuller Evangelistic Association, Department of Church Growth, Box 989, Pasadena, California 91102 is recommended.
15. James A. Davey, "How to Discover Your Spiritual Gift," *Christianity Today* (Carol Stream, Illinois, May 9, 1975), p. 9.
16. Charles Mylander, "How to Discover Your Spiritual Gifts," *Eternity* (May 1973), p. 27.
17. Romans 11:29 *(NASB)*.
18. James A. Davey, *op. cit.*, p. 11.

Chapter Eleven
1. A. A. Milne, *Winnie the Pooh.*
2. *The Poems of Emily Dickenson* (New York: T. Y. Crowell, 1964), p. 20.

Chapter Thirteen
1. Rene Padilla in *Let the Earth Hear His Voice,* ed. J. D. Douglas (Minneapolis: Worldwide Publications, 1975), p. 128.
2. Phyllis McGinley, *Sixpence in Her Shoe* (New York: Dell Pub. Co., 1965), pp. 80-81.

3. John R. W. Stott, *Christian Mission in the Modern World* (Downers Grove, Ill.: InterVarsity Press, 1975), pp. 34-35.
4. Os Guinness, *In Two Minds* (Downers Grove, Ill.: InterVarsity Press, 1976), p. 121.
5. Ronald J. Sider, *Rich Christians in an Age of Hunger* (Downers Grove, Ill.: InterVarsity Press, 1977), p. 187.
6. Dom Helder Camara, *Revolution through Peace* (New York: Harper & Row, 1971).